Great Voyages

DARING ADVENTURERS
FROM JAMES COOK TO GERTRUDE BELL

Deborah Patterson

Introduction

When Marco Polo set off on his epic journey from Venice, Italy in 1271, a map of the world looked like this.

By the time Neil Armstrong and Buzz Aldrin landed on the Moon in 1969, a map of the world looked like this and, more than that, we'd mapped most of the solar system and made a start on mapping the known universe!

First published 2018 by
The British Library
96 Euston Road
London NW1 2DB

Text © Deborah Patterson 2018
Illustrations © British Library Board and other named copyright-holders 2018
ISBN 978 0 7123 5285 7

British Library Cataloguing-in-Publication data
A catalogue record for this publication is available from the British Library

Designed by Goldust Design
Picture research by Sally Nicholls
Printed in China by
C&C Offset Printing Co.

Adventurers have always gone that one step further in pursuit of their dreams, braving extremes of weather, exhaustion and discomfort to discover more about our world. Marco Polo endured baking hot days and freezing nights as he travelled through the Gobi Desert on his way from medieval Italy to China. Ferdinand Magellan braved waves as big as mountains in unknown oceans in his small wooden ship. 21st century astronauts space walk outside the International Space Station.

Adventurers have travelled in pursuit of knowledge. Gaps on the map of the world have been filled in thanks to them, and they've gathered information that helps us understand how the world works and learn what lives on it. Some brave explorers have been sent on a mission by their country to claim a new land or open up a new trade route. Others set their own targets and embarked on their journeys for the glory. They wanted to return home heroes and be the first to achieve something extraordinary.

Whatever the reasons behind their journeys, these great explorers have opened up the world to the rest of us.

ARE YOU READY TO EXPLORE WITH US?

So put on your walking shoes, pack your bags and get ready to follow in the footsteps of history's most DARING ADVENTURERS!

where in the world?

Searching for the Northwest Passage
The frozen seas of northern Canada presented a challenge to a number of brave explorers, who tried to find a way through the ice floes to Asia in the 16th and 17th centuries. Wrap up warm to read their stories from **page 34**.

Discovering the Wild West
Join Meriwether Lewis and William Clark on **page 58** for an expedition into the untamed wilderness of North America. Watch out for bears!

Admiral of the Oceans
In 1492 Columbus sailed the ocean blue... Turn to **page 22** to find out more about the man and his unexpected discovery of a new world.

Pirate on the High Seas
On **page 40** join Francis Drake as he sails around the world, annoying the Spanish and looting lots of treasure along the way.

The Voyage of the Beagle
A young naturalist, Charles Darwin, joined the *Beagle* on its journey to South America in 1831. Be part of the crew on **page 64**.

SO YOU WANT TO BE AN EXPLORER?
If you're ready for an adventure of your own, learn some top tips from modern-day explorers on **page 94**.

Magellan's Voyage
On **page 28** read about the extraordinary story of the first voyage around the world, and the surprise of who actually made it (spoiler alert – it wasn't Ferdinand Magellan!).

A Pioneering Woman
Have you heard of Maria Sibylla Merian? No? Well turn to **page 46** to discover the story of her groundbreaking rainforest adventure.

Marco Polos Adventures
Join Marco Polo on his adventure from medieval Venice to the Far East on **page 6**.

The Desert Queen
Gertrude Bell faced sandstorms and violent desert tribes in pursuit of her passions for archaeology and Arabia. Follow in her footsteps on **page 76**.

To the Moon
Take a step into the unknown with Neil Armstrong and Buzz Aldrin on **page 88** as they land on the Moon.

A City at Sea
Imagine commanding a fleet of ships carrying 28,000 men. That's just what Zheng He did for the Chinese Emperor. Discover more on **page 18**.

Into Africa
Does a lion's roar reduce you to jelly? Do you scream at the sight of a crocodile? If not then you might just be brave enough to step into Africa with David Livingstone on **page 70**.

The Longest Journey
Ibn Battuta left his home in Tangier in 1325 and travelled for 24 years. Find out why on **page 12**.

Captain Cook's Voyage of Discovery
Secret orders from King George III led Captain James Cook further south than any previous explorer. Join him on his historic voyage on **page 52**.

The Imperial Trans-Antarctic Expedition
Put on your best cold-weather gear to join Ernest Shackleton's crew aboard the *Endurance* on its hazardous Antarctic expedition on **page 82**.

Marco Polo's Adventures

In 1271 Marco Polo joined his father and uncle on a trade trip from Venice to China. He didn't know then that he would be away from home for more than twenty years.

Trip of a lifetime

In 1260 Marco Polo's father, Niccolo, and uncle, Mafeo, left Venice on a trading expedition to the east. By 1266 they had got as far as Cambulac, known now as Beijing. This was the location of the Chinese court from where Kublai Khan, also known as the 'Great Khan', governed China. They returned to Europe in 1269 as ambassadors of the Great Khan with hopes to travel east again one day.

That day came in 1271 when Niccolo and Mafeo set off once again, joined this time by 17-year-old Marco.

A MEDIEVAL MARITIME EMPIRE
Venice is a city in Italy that's famous now for its canals and gondolas, but in the 13th century it was a prosperous trade port. It was the commercial centre of the Mediterranean and the starting point for many trips east, where Venetian merchants sought out luxury Asian goods such as silk and spices.

It took nearly four years to get from Venice to China. They travelled first to Constantinople, then headed south-east where they had planned to sail to China from Hormuz in the Persian Gulf. The ships available didn't meet the Polos' standards, however, and they decided not to risk the sea route. So the travellers continued their journey overland.

This image dates back to about 1410. It's from a French version of Marco Polo's book, *The Description of the World*, and shows Niccolo, Mafeo and Marco Polo arriving at the port of Hormuz on the Gulf of Persia.

THE BOLD LINE ON THIS MAP SHOWS MARCO POLO'S ROUTE.

They probably travelled by horse, with camels carrying their items for the Khan and their belongings. It was an incredibly tough trek which took the explorers through the Pamir mountain range, an area that today is often referred to as 'the roof of the world', the shifting sands of the Taklamakan Desert and the searing hot days and freezing cold nights of the Gobi Desert.

THIS DESCRIPTION OF THE GOBI DESERT WAS WRITTEN IN MARCO POLO'S BOOK, *THE DESCRIPTION OF THE WORLD*.

'It consists entirely of mountains and sand and valleys. There is nothing at all to eat. And all the way through the desert for a day and a night before you find water. Beasts and birds there are none, because they find nothing to eat.'

Overcoming obstacles

This was a very hard journey across challenging terrain for the Polos, so it's not surprising it took them a long time to reach China. At one point, before they even reached the Pamir Mountains, the explorers were forced to stop for nearly a year due to illness. After making it safely across the Gobi they spent a year in Suchow (present-day Dunhuang) before finally arriving at their destination, the Great Khan's summer court in northern China in 1275.

Homeward bound

In 1292, nearly twenty years after they'd left Venice, the Polos decided to return home. They had one last task to complete for the Great Khan on the way. They were asked to accompany a Mongol princess to Persia (present-day Iran) to marry a prince. The Polos took the sea route home, passing by coastal China, south-east Asia and the Spice Islands before rounding the southern-most tip of India and crossing the Persian Gulf to arrive in Hormuz. From there it was a relatively easy and well trodden route back to Venice.

WHEN MARCO POLO WAS ALIVE, NORTHERN CHINA WAS KNOWN AS CATHAY BY EUROPEANS.

THE SILK ROAD

Long before Niccolo and Mafeo Polo set off on their first trip east, trade routes were established connecting China with the Middle East, India and Europe. This network of routes became known as the Silk Road because one of the main products traded was the luxurious silk made by the Chinese.

The Chinese had traded silk to the Roman Empire from as early as the 1st century BC. In return they received wool, silver and gold from the Europeans. However, with the decline of the Roman Empire in the 4th century, the Silk Road fell out of use. By the 13th century, when the Polos lived in Venice, the trade routes were being revived again.

It would have been rare for a single merchant to travel the entire length of the route, from the Mediterranean ports, across the Pamir Mountains, alongside the Great Wall of China and all the way to Xi'an, Shanghai and Beijing. Instead, the goods being traded would have been passed to a middleman. This person would have carried the items to a staging post, where they would have been passed to another middleman and so on until they reached their final destination. When Niccolo and Mafeo reached the Chinese court in 1266 they would have been among the very first Europeans to experience Chinese culture.

Information was traded along the Silk Road as well as products. The route was important for sharing knowledge, ideas and religion between cultures. Bacteria may also have been passed unknowingly among the traders. Some scientists think it may have been the way that the Black Death spread from Europe to Asia.

The Polo brothers and the Great Khan.

Adventures in China

Marco Polo was excellent at languages and impressed the Great Khan with his intelligence and knowledge. The Khan was the head of the vast Mongol Empire and decided to employ Marco Polo as a sort of spy. Polo was sent to the far corners of the Khan's empire, which extended across China, as well as to Burma and India. His role was to gather information about the places and people he encountered. He also served as a tax inspector in Yanzhou for three years. Polo worked for the emperor for a total of 17 years.

This map of China is just a small part of a much larger map of the world. It was drawn by an Italian monk, Fra. Mauro, in 1459. The grand city that you can see is Beijing.

? HOW DO WE KNOW WHAT WE KNOW?

Marco Polo's journey was extraordinary but not much more so than the voyages taken by his father and uncle, so why is Marco famous, but not his dad?

Three years after Polo arrived back in Venice he was sent to prison. His cellmate was an author called Rustichello da Pisa. Polo told da Pisa the stories of his twenty-three year trip away from Venice, and those stories were eventually gathered together to create a book called *The Description of the World*.

The book captured the public imagination. It's not hard to understand why. This was probably the first time a European had written about the exotic Far East. It was also the last time a major text would be written about China for centuries. Christopher Columbus had a copy of the book with him when he set out across the Atlantic, searching for China, and even 19th century explorers such as Marc Aurel Stein referred to *The Travels of Marco Polo* to help plan their routes.

While he was in China, Polo was one of the first Europeans to set eyes on such items as paper money and asbestos. His accounts of these new things, including **coal**, can all be found in his book along with details of the people and places he came across.

DID YOU KNOW?

Marco Polo and Rustichello da Pisa's book, *The Description of the World*, is most often known in English-speaking countries as *The Travels of Marco Polo*. It is also known in Italian as *Il Milione (The Million)*, which was the nickname Marco was given as a result of the amazing number of facts he shared about the Great Khan's vast court.

'It is a fact that all over the country of Cathay there is a kind of black stone existing in beds in the mountains, which they dig out and burn like firewood.'

This image of Mongolian messengers in Somalia is from a French version of *The Description of the World* published in about 1410.

Do you believe everything you read?

When it was published *The Travels of Marco Polo* became a bestseller, but not everyone was a fan of the book. Many said that it was full of exaggerations and outright lies. Some suggested that Polo hadn't even been to China. In 1324, when he was dying, an attempt was made to get him to confess to telling "a pack of lies". Polo's response was to say that he had "only told you half of what I know".

We now know that much of what was written down in the book was true, such as the use of paper money and the production of iron, but we can also see that he didn't mention the Great Wall or the Chinese practice of foot binding, which is surprising. The question remains, did Polo actually go to China? What do you think?

The Longest Journey

In 1325 Ibn Battuta set out on a religious pilgrimage on his own. The journey to Mecca and back should have taken him just eighteen months but the desire to continue his travels was too strong, and he didn't return home to Tangier for 24 years.

VOYAGE FACTS

When: 1325–1349

Where: From Tangier, Morocco, to Hangzhou, near Shanghai, China, and many places in between

How: Overland and by sea

Why: Like a modern-day tourist, Ibn Battuta travelled to see new places and experience different cultures

Who: Battuta started out alone, but returned home with wives, followers and servants

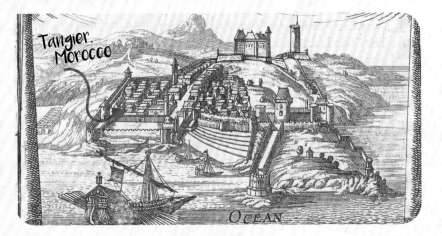

Tangier, Morocco

OCEAN

Who was Ibn Battuta?

Ibn Battuta came from a family of judges of Islamic law, known as *qadis*. They were a well respected family in his home town of Tangier, Morocco. Though he was reluctant to leave his parents, he was very keen to make the hajj, a Muslim pilgrimage to Mecca in present-day Saudi Arabia. In June 1325, when he was only 21 years old, Battuta left home on his own to start his pilgrimage. He had been studying Islamic law as a young man and planned to continue his studies, as much as possible, with well respected Sufi scholars in the Middle East.

He reached the holy city of Mecca in October 1326 and was inspired by seeing Muslims from so many different countries in one place. It made him realise that even though he had already travelled nearly 4,000 miles (6,400km), there was a lot more of the world to see, and he wanted to see it. Battuta had one aim as a traveller, and that was 'never to travel any road a second time'.

THE HAJJ

The hajj is the Muslim pilgrimage to Mecca that takes place each year. Every Muslim must make the hajj at least once in their lives if they are physically able and can afford it. When Ibn Battuta was alive, pilgrims would have met in various cities and then travelled to Mecca together. Ibn Battuta made the hajj seven times in total. These days around two million Muslims make the pilgrimage to Mecca each year.

THIS VIEW OF PILGRIMS IN MECCA DATES BACK TO AROUND THE YEAR 1410.

The original tourist

After completing his first pilgrimage to Mecca, Ibn Battuta began his travels in earnest. He wanted to see as much of the known world as possible. From Mecca he set out across the Arabian Desert to Baghdad and then Persia before returning to the holy city. He hadn't seen enough yet, so he then sailed down the East African coast to Mombasa in present-day Kenya, before heading back north. This time, however, the explorer continued north to the Black Sea, then Crimea and the Caucasus. The extreme cold sent him searching for the sun again, and he headed to Constantinople (today's Istanbul) and then east to Afghanistan and India. Battuta stayed in India for eight years before going to China, travelling mainly by boat.

Even after he returned home to Tangier in 1349, Battuta couldn't stay still. Two more journeys followed – the first was just a short hop to Andalusia in southern Spain and the second, an expedition across the Sahara to Timbuktu.

THIS PAINTING OF THE SANCTUARY AT MECCA IS FROM A 17TH CENTURY PERSIAN MANUSCRIPT.

A working holiday

Luckily for Ibn Battuta, his training as a *qadi* made him a very well respected person in the Islamic lands that he visited, and also helped him to get jobs to fund his travels. Sultan Muhammed Tughlaq of Delhi employed him as a *qadi* before sending him to China as his ambassador. He was also employed as a *qadi* on the Maldive Islands.

Though he had set out on his hajj alone at the age of 21, he quickly met other pilgrims, and after that, he almost always had company. By the time he reached India, a harem of wives travelled with him and he had gained an entourage of followers.

When he finished his travels, Battuta wrote a book about everything he had seen and done. It was called *Gift to Observers, Dealing with the Curiosities of Cities and the Wonders of Journeys* or *Rihla* (Travels). It's now known as *Travels in Asia and Africa, 1325–1354*.

IBN BATTUTA WOULD HAVE SAILED THE RED SEA AND THE INDIAN OCEAN ON A DHOW, A TYPE OF ARAB SAILBOAT STILL USED TODAY.

DREAM TRIP

HAVE YOU EVER DREAMT OF TRAVELLING TO A DIFFERENT COUNTRY?

Ibn Battuta had a dream of being carried eastwards on the back of a huge bird. He believed this was a sign that he should travel to the Muslim countries to the east. Perhaps he was also having a premonition about travelling in an aeroplane! It would have been easier than walking or going on the back of a donkey.

THE ISLAMIC WORLD

Ibn Battuta was travelling at a time when a large part of the known world, from Spain and North Africa to India, Central Asia and Java (in present-day Indonesia) was Islamic. As he was a Muslim, that meant he was able to travel through these countries fairly easily. He did travel in non-Muslim countries too and wrote about the differences in culture he found there.

THE MAP BELOW, BY HANNA BALICKA FRIBES, SHOWS IBN BATTUTA'S ROUTE.

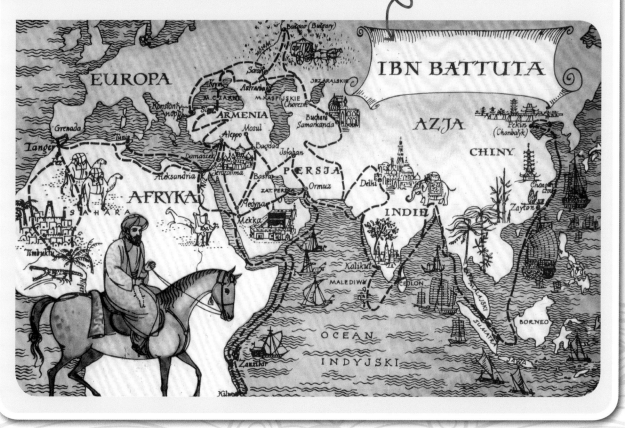

TRY IT — YOU MIGHT LIKE IT!

When we travel to different countries, we often find ourselves eating unfamiliar food or drinking something unusual. It was the same for Ibn Battuta who had to try everything he was offered by his hosts. If he hadn't, he would have offended them. He wrote this description of trying something new in his book, *Travels in Asia and Africa, 1325–1354*.

'...I visited the principal Khátún Taytughl, who is the queen and the mother of the sultan's two sons. The Khátún had a golden tray filled with cherries in front of her and was cleaning them. She ordered qumizz to be brought and with her own hand poured out a cupful and gave it to me, which is the highest of honours in their estimation. I had never drunk qumizz before, but there was nothing for me but to accept it. I tasted it, but found it disagreeable and passed it on to one of my companions.'

So what had he been given to drink that he found so 'disagreeable'? *Qumizz*, also known as kumis, is an alcoholic drink made from fermented horse's milk. Mmmm, delicious!

THIS DRAWING SHOWS IBN BATTUTA IN EGYPT. HE SPENT A MONTH IN CAIRO ON HIS WAY TO MECCA.

Travel troubles

In 1342 the Sultan Muhammed Tughlaq in Delhi, India, sent Battuta as his ambassador to China with some gifts for the Chinese emperor. On this journey he and his entourage were attacked. Battuta was captured and almost executed. He escaped death, and continued his journey only to be shipwrecked on the Malabar coast. He lost everything – the gifts for the emperor and all of his possessions. Battuta was an experienced traveller, however, and was not put off by these setbacks so he continued on to China. Thankfully, after these experiences, he found China to be 'the safest and best regulated of countries for a traveller'.

IBN BATTUTA TRAVELLED A TOTAL OF 75,000 MILES (120,000KM). THAT'S EQUIVALENT TO GOING AROUND THE WORLD THREE TIMES!

A TYPICAL ARAB SAILING BOAT FROM THE 13TH CENTURY.

A City at Sea

Admiral Zheng He led a fleet of ships on seven separate voyages at the command of Emperor Yongle of China. The plan was to replace well trodden overland trade routes with shipping routes.

VOYAGE FACTS

When: 1405–1433

Where: Seven voyages from China to India, Arabia, Indonesia and Africa

How: With a fleet of ships known as junks

Why: At the command of Emperor Yongle to trade and extend Chinese influence

Who: Zheng He and up to 28,000 men

Who was Zheng He?

Zheng He was the greatest Chinese explorer of his time but he had humble beginnings. He was born into a Hui (Chinese Muslim) family in the Yunnan province. In 1381, when he was about ten years old, the soldiers of the Chinese Ming dynasty overthrew the last Mongol stronghold in China and captured young boys, including Zheng He. After they were captured, these boys were forced to work in the Chinese army.

Zheng He did a good job when he was in the army, and was noticed by the men in charge. He became very influential in the Chinese court and was eventually selected by Emperor Yongle to be commander-in-chief of a series of expeditions to 'Western Oceans'.

DID YOU KNOW?

When Zheng He was born he was called Ma He. It was Prince Zhu Di, who later became Emperor Yongle, who gave him the name Zheng. If this isn't confusing enough, he's also sometimes known as Cheng Ho!

Who's the boss?

EMPEROR YONGLE

When Emperor Yongle came to power, many of the overland trade routes, which the Chinese had traditionally relied upon, had been destroyed by the Mongol Empire. He wanted to set up safe shipping routes to enable China to continue to trade. At the same time, the emperor wanted to make sure the overseas ports China traded with understood how strong and important the Ming Empire was.

The size of the fleet – and the size of the treasure ships, which were much larger than any European ship of the time – was designed to show off China's wealth and influence. It seemed to work because the fleet was apparently welcomed in most of the places it visited. It helped that the fleet presented local rulers with gifts. However, there were a few places where Zheng He decided that he needed to use force to make sure the locals understood exactly who was in charge.

HOW DID THEY FIND THEIR WAY?

The Chinese were ahead of the game when it came to seafaring and navigation. It's thought that they invented the compass as early as the 8th century, perhaps even earlier, so it's likely that Zheng He used one on his sea voyages.

A magnetic compass is used by a navigator to determine which way is north. It uses the Earth's natural magnetism to point to the magnetic North Pole. Once the navigator knows where north is, they can work out any other direction they need.

TREASURE SHIPS

The largest of Zheng He's ships were known as *bao chuan*, or treasure ships. They were almost 140m (450ft) long. That's as long as fourteen double-decker buses!

It's no wonder the ships were known as treasure ships. This is a list of some of the items that Zheng He brought back to China from his travels.

Rhinocerous horn
Ivory
Tortoiseshell
Rare woods
Incense
Spices
Medicines
Pearls
Precious stones
A giraffe

Bigger is better!

Zheng He led a total of seven voyages, beginning with an expedition to Calicut (present-day Kozhikode) in Kerala on India's west coast. A fleet of sixty-three ocean-going junks, carrying a total of 28,000 men – including scientists, doctors, translators, administrators, seamen and soldiers – and a large cargo of porcelain, silk and other Chinese products, set sail from the mouth of the Yangtze River. Nothing of this scale had ever been seen on the ocean before.

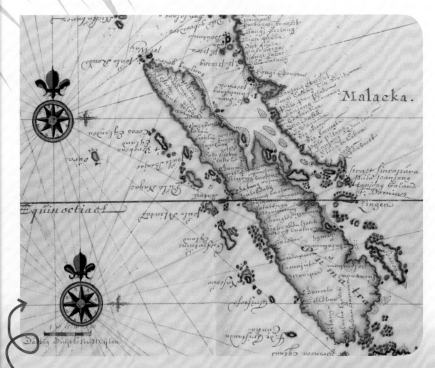

A 17TH CENTURY DUTCH MAP OF MALACCA AND SUMATRA.

On Zheng He's first expedition, the fleet called at Java, Aceh, on the island of Sumatra and Sri Lanka before reaching Calicut on India's west coast. This expedition was seen to be a success by the emperor, who then decided to fund further voyages. Zheng He went to Calicut again then, between 1409 and 1415, he led expeditions to Hormuz in the Middle East and Jeddah on the Red Sea. His next few voyages took him to Malacca in Malaysia, then Mogadishu and Malindi on Africa's east coast. His final voyage, made between 1430 and 1433, took him back to Hormuz. He died shortly after completing this voyage and was buried at sea.

? HOW DO WE KNOW WHAT WE KNOW?

The emperor sent a translator, Ma Huan, with Zheng He on three of the voyages. As well as translating for the admiral, Ma Huan also took notes about the places they visited. He eventually collected all of these notes together to make a book called *The Overall Survey of the Ocean's Shores*.

A SWASH-BUCKLING BATTLE

On the way home from his first trip to Calicut, Zheng He encountered the fierce pirate, Ch'en Tsu'i. A great battle followed. Zheng He was victorious after killing five thousand of the enemy sailors. Ch'en Tsu'i was taken prisoner and transported back to Nanjing where he was executed.

PICTURE THIS...

Imagine standing on the coast of your country, where you might normally spot small fishing boats and the occasional ferry. Instead, you see a fleet of around 300 hundred huge ships on the horizon, heading straight for your port. The size and scale of Admiral Zheng's fleet would have seemed like a city rising out of the waves.

Admiral of the Oceans

Christopher Columbus set sail into the unknown, expecting to find a sea route to Asia. Instead he discovered a whole new world.

VOYAGE FACTS

When: 3 August 1492 to 12 October 1492 (first landfall)

Where: Palos, Spain to the Bahamas

How: 3 ships – the *Santa Maria*, the *Pinta* and the *Niña*

Why: To sail to Asia

Who: Christopher Columbus and 90 crewmen

CHRISTOPHER COLUMBUS, PAINTED BY SEBASTIANO DEL PIOMBO, 1519.

Make the facts fit

Christopher Columbus, a captain from Genoa, Italy, believed that it would be possible to reach Asia by sailing west from Europe. He did a lot of research, looking at many maps and descriptions of the known world. He believed that the world was about 20% smaller than most people thought it was at that time and he even drew a map to show this. He was confident he could make the journey to Asia by sea, he just needed some money. Queen Isabella of Spain decided to back him and so began one of the most famous expeditions of all time.

Sailing the ocean blue

On 3 August 1492, Columbus set off across the Atlantic Ocean. This was a time when people living in Europe didn't know that the continents of North and South America existed. Columbus truly believed that if he continued to sail west he would eventually reach Asia. He had no idea of the vast landmass that would mark the end of his journey.

Can you imagine not knowing exactly which way you are travelling, and not really knowing how long you're going to be at sea? That's what faced the crews of the *Santa Maria*, the *Pinta* and the *Niña*, the ships that sailed under the leadership of Columbus. It's not surprising that many of the crew were frightened and ready to turn back for home after spending many weeks at sea without seeing any sign of land.

THE ATLANTIC OCEAN WAS SOMETIMES KNOWN AS THE GREEN SEA OF DARKNESS!

HOW DID THEY FIND THEIR WAY?

Columbus did have navigational instruments on board his ships, and he knew how to use the stars to navigate, but instead it appears that he relied on 'dead reckoning'. This is a navigational technique that involves calculating a ship's position by estimating the distance travelled in a particular direction from a specific point. Incredibly this proved to be very successful for Columbus. The course he took was very similar to the ideal transatlantic shipping route used by voyagers for many years afterwards.

This is the *Santa Maria*, Columbus's largest ship. The *Santa Maria* was a carrack, a three-masted vessel suitable for sailing the ocean. The other ships were caravels, which were smaller and more manoeuvrable sailing ships.

We've arrived! I think?

On 11 October 1492, after spending about two months at sea, land was finally sighted and, a day later, they stepped off their ships on to solid ground. The place they had reached wasn't in Asia, as Christopher Columbus believed, but was an island in what we now call the Bahamas. Columbus named the island San Salvador and claimed it for Spain.

When they arrived, Columbus and his crew came into contact with some locals, known as the Taino people. Their first encounters with each other were friendly and gifts were exchanged.

Believing that he had reached the 'East Indies', Columbus referred to the local people as Indios, or Indians. The islands of the Carribean that Columbus explored on his first voyage are still known as the West Indies today.

'Soon many people of the island gathered there...to some of them I gave red caps and glass beads which they put on their chests and many other things of small value...'

FIRST IMPRESSIONS OF THE LOCALS IN *COLUMBUS'S DIARIES* BY BARTOLOMÉ DE LAS CASAS

THIS MAP OF THE WEST INDIES, DRAWN BY THEODOR DE BRY IN 1594, SHOWS THE PLACES THAT CHRISTOPHER COLUMBUS DISCOVERED. CAN YOU SPOT HAITI? WHAT OTHER FAMILIAR PLACES CAN YOU SEE?

Exploring the West Indies

In the months that followed his arrival in the Bahamas, Columbus and his men explored the local islands and some of the coast of Cuba. Columbus also sailed close to a large island that he called La Española, or Hispaniola. This island now consists of the countries Haiti and the Dominican Republic.

It was here that Columbus's trip narrowly avoided disaster. On Christmas Day 1492 a storm hit and the *Santa Maria* got into difficulty. Luckily, the crew were helped by a local king, Guacanagari. Their cargo was safely offloaded by locals and the ship avoided being capsized. They discovered gold on the island of La Española and so Columbus built a settlement there, calling it La Navidad. He returned to Europe leaving 40 crew members behind in the settlement.

Columbus sailed back to Spain in triumph, believing that he had reached the east, and carried with him a cargo of gold and cotton to present to the royal court. The King and Queen of Spain were delighted and gave him the grand title Admiral of the Oceans.

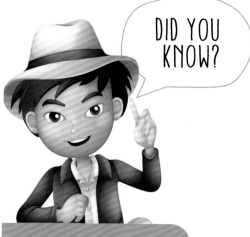

DID YOU KNOW?

Columbus returned to the Americas three more times, and continued to believe until the day he died that he was exploring the east coast of Asia.

A Caribbean nightmare

It wasn't all smooth sailing for the Spaniards who attempted to make their home in the new world. When Columbus returned to La Navidad less than a year after he'd left 40 men there, he discovered that they had been massacred by the natives. Columbus set up a new colony called Santo Domingo and gave his brother, Bartholomeo, the job of governor. Over time the colonists realised that food was hard to come by while the gold they were supposed to be mining was even harder to get their hands on. They rose up against their governor, who suppressed this mutiny with great force, hanging some of the mutineers. Both the Columbus brothers were arrested for these actions, a fall from grace from which Christopher never really recovered.

The VIKINGS were here

Around 400 years before Columbus reached North America, a group of Vikings, led by Leif Eriksson, son of the legendary Erik the Red, sailed west from Greenland. These early explorers landed in a number of places on a search for new, fertile land to settle, including the present-day Baffin and Labrador Islands in Canada. It's possible that they even sailed as far south as Nantucket, Massachusetts, in North America. Eriksson saw grapes growing on vines in Massachusetts and named this new land Vinland.

The Vikings did not establish a permanent settlement in these new lands, perhaps because the locals were hostile or because the climate was too harsh, and their discovery remained a secret to other Europeans for centuries to come.

ISLAND OF TERCERA IN THE AZORES.

Blown away

Before setting off on his Caribbean adventure on behalf of Spain, Columbus had already spent many years sailing for the Portuguese in the Atlantic Ocean and was familiar with the winds found there. He knew the north-east trade winds already and felt confident that they would push his ships west across the ocean. Columbus also knew of the 'westerlies' but didn't know where they originated. He guessed that they blew from the land that he was headed for, and would be able to bring the ships back to Spain. Happily for the two ships that made the journey home, he was proved right. Striking out east for home from the Caribbean in January 1493, he found the 'westerlies' and reached the familiar waters of the Azores about a month later.

EAST IS EAST

Five years after Columbus travelled west, Vasco de Gama sailed south and led the first voyage to successfully sail past the tip of Africa. In doing so a shipping route to the east was finally established.

Magellan's Voyage

Ferdinand Magellan attempted to reach the Spice Islands by sailing west from Spain instead of east. This bold challenge led to the first round-the-world trip.

VOYAGE FACTS

When: 1519–1522

Where: From Spain via South America to the Spice Islands

How: Five wooden sailing ships

Why: To claim the Spice Islands for the Spanish Empire

Who: Ferdinand Magellan with a crew of 241 men

Who was Magellan?

Ferdinand Magellan was Portuguese, and a great adventurer and navigator. Before his infamous round-the-world voyage attempt, he had fought against the Moors in Morocco, visited Malaysia and been injured fighting in India.

Spain vs Portugal

The rivalry between Spain and Portugal was legendary. In the early 1500s they both wanted control of a small group of islands in the Indonesian archipelago called the Moluccas. These small, out-of-the-way islands were known as the Spice Islands because of their cloves and nutmeg, which were two of the most popular and highly valued spices of the day.

Nutmeg

In 1494 the Spanish and Portuguese governments agreed to the Treaty of Tordesillas, which divided the 'New World' between the two countries. On a map of the world, an imaginary line was drawn, north to south, cutting straight through Brazil. To the west of that line it was agreed that all of the countries could be claimed by Spain. This included present-day Mexico, Chile and Colombia. Portugal could claim the countries to the east.

SPAIN   PORTUGAL

TREATY OF TORDESILLAS LINE.

These included present-day Brazil but also, importantly for the spice trade, the Moluccas. This line didn't account for the possibility of sailing west though, past the tip of South America, and reaching the Spice Islands by crossing the Pacific Ocean. The Spanish were determined to claim these islands for themselves, so they set out to chart a new course around the world.

THE SHIPS

Magellan's expedition left Spain in five wooden sailing vessels. The flagship, the *Trinidad*, carrying Magellan, was a carrack, as were the *Victoria*, the *San Antonio* and the *Concepción*. The *Santiago* was a caravel, a smaller ship. Not all of the ships managed to make the full journey. Before they had rounded the tip of South America, the *Santiago* filled with water and sank. The crew of the *San Antonio* simply decided not to continue on the hazardous journey and turned back, taking with it most of the food stores needed by the expedition.

THESE PEOPLE ARE BUILDING A CARAVEL.

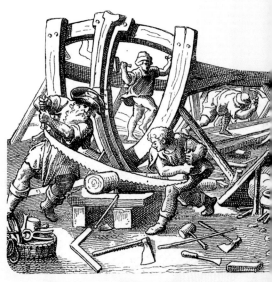

The Magellan Strait

In September 1519 Magellan and his men left Seville in Spain and set out across the Atlantic Ocean towards the tip of South America. At this time it wasn't known if the landmass of South America stretched all the way to the South Pole. If it did, ships simply wouldn't be able to get through. Magellan and his flotilla of small ships sailed for a full year, surviving thunderstorms and an attempted mutiny by some of the sailors (Magellan executed one of leaders of this uprising and left the other marooned on the coast) before they came across a potential passageway through, as described by one of their crew members.

'...on approaching the end of the bay, and thinking they were lost, they saw a small opening which did not appear to be an opening but a sharp turn. Like desperate men they hauled into it, and thus they discovered the strait by chance.'

NAMESAKES

The tricky passage from the Atlantic to the Pacific Ocean through which Magellan and his expedition struggled is now named the Strait of Magellan. As he sailed past the tip of South America, Magellan spotted small birds swimming in the sea. These are now called Magellanic penguins.

THE CHALLENGING STRAIT OF MAGELLAN, WHICH MAGELLAN AND HIS EXHAUSTED CREWS SAILED THROUGH IN 1520.

Navigating through this strait proved to be a greater challenge than any of the men could have expected. It twisted its way through the snow-covered mountains and a cold wind whipped through the narrow passage. It took the men 38 days to make their way through. Imagine their relief as they entered the relatively calm waters of the ocean on the other side. It's said that Magellan wept with relief and named the ocean the Pacific.

PACIFICO MEANS PEACEFUL IN SPANISH AND PORTUGUESE.

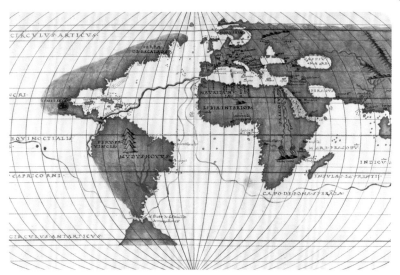

Flat or round?

It used to be thought that the Earth was flat. Early Greek maps from around 600BC show the world as a flattened disc surrounded by sea. Over time this view came to be challenged and, by the time Columbus discovered the Americas in 1492, it was generally accepted that the world was round.

Once they knew the world was round, mariners and navigators wanted to circumnavigate it, that is, sail all the way around the globe. Without detailed maps to work on, these early navigators were setting themselves the greatest challenge of their time.

SCOURGE OF SCURVY

– or why you should always eat your five a day

Magellan mistakenly thought that once he'd made his way past the continent of South America, it would only take him around three days to reach the Moluccas. In fact, it took more than three months to make landfall. The sailors had no provisions left. They ate 'powder of biscuits swarming with worms' and rats, if they could catch them.

Many suffered and even died from scurvy, a disease caused by a lack of vitamin C, which we can get from eating fruit and vegetables, especially citrus fruit. Unfortunately for the sailors on Magellan's ships, and on many other great sea voyages, the cause of scurvy wasn't discovered until the 1930s.

The ships did eventually reach the Spice Islands and collected their precious cargo of cloves and nutmeg before sailing back to Spain.

The first circumnavigator

Magellan himself didn't actually make it all the way around the world. Sadly, he died on the Philippine island of Cebu. Sebastian d'Elcano, who was in charge of the expedition on its successful homeward journey, was the first person to go around the world in a single expedition. However, the honour of being the first ever circumnavigator of the globe goes the expedition's Moluccan slave, Enrique. He had been taken from the Moluccas several years earlier but his voyage on Magellan's expedition took him back to those islands – the long way round.

ONE OF THE CREW MEMBERS, ANTONIO PIGAFETTA, DESCRIBED MAGELLAN'S DEATH IN HIS BOOK, *FIRST VOYAGE AROUND THE WORLD*:

'An Indian hurled a bamboo spear into the captains face, but the latter immediately killed him with his lance, which he left in the Indians body. Then, trying to lay hand on sword, he could draw it out but halfway, because he had been wounded in the arm with a bamboo spear. When the natives saw that, they all hurled themselves upon him.'

OTHER SUCCESSFUL EARLY CIRCUMNAVIGATORS

Francis Drake (1577–80)
Olivier van Noort (1588–1601)
William Dampier (1678–91, 1703 and 1708–11)

In the 21st century, the world has been circumnavigated in many different ways, from sailing and rowing to flying in a hot-air balloon. Do you fancy giving it a try?

AS EXPLORERS DISCOVERED MORE OF THE WORLD, CARTOGRAPHERS (MAP-MAKERS) WERE KEPT BUSY. THIS MAP OF THE PACIFIC OCEAN AND SURROUNDING COUNTRIES BY ABRAHAM ORTELIUS WAS COMPLETED IN 1589 AND SHOWS MAGELLAN'S SHIP CROSSING THE OCEAN.

Searching for the Northwest Passage

European sailors knew that the great landmass of North and South America lay between them and the Pacific Ocean, but they were determined to find a way through. From 1576 to 1631 this search focused on the Northwest Passage.

FROBISHER

VOYAGE FACTS

When: Eight attempts between 1576 and 1631

Where: In the frozen seas of northern Canada

How: Small wooden sailing boats

Why: Looking for a northerly sea route to China

Who: Frobisher (1576, 1577 and 1578), Davis (1585 and 1587), Hudson (1610), Baffin (1616 and 1631)

Destination China

Sailors and navigators had been trying to find an easy way to reach the Spice Islands and China from Europe for hundreds of years. Progress had been made, with Vasco de Gama successfully battling the winds and currents to sail past the tip of Africa in 1497, and Magellan making his way through a treacherous route at the very bottom of South America in 1520, but still the search was on.

It was assumed that there would be a way to sail to China from Europe by going across the top of the continent of North America, using a series of seas, bays and waterways. This route came to be known as the Northwest Passage. This wasn't to be an easy task. The brave explorers who attempted this journey would face unimaginable dangers from pack ice, hostile locals and freezing temperatures.

Baffin Island

This map, from a 1578 book, shows the area that Frobisher explored in his search for the entrance to the Northwest Passage.

Gold or glory?

Martin Frobisher was an English navigator and explorer who wanted to take up the challenge of finding the Northwest Passage. His first voyage was backed by the Company of Cathay (the old English word for China). He crossed the Atlantic in 1576 in a small ship called *Gabriel* with a crew of only eighteen men. On the south-east coast of Baffin Island, he found an opening from which a strong tide of water rushed out. It was thought that this might be the entrance to the passage but, before they explored any further, Frobisher's men came to him with the exciting news that they had found gold! He returned to England with a dream of making it rich and planned his return trips.

Frobisher sailed back to the area twice, in 1577 and 1578. His third and final voyage was by far his biggest, with a fleet of 15 ships. The ships were loaded with the precious minerals and taken back to England. Unfortunately for Frobisher, his sparkling cargo turned out to be iron pyrites, a worthless mineral known as 'fool's gold'.

THE OPENING THAT FROBISHER FOUND NEAR BAFFIN ISLAND WAS LATER NAMED FROBISHER BAY.

A frozen obstacle course

If you look at a map of the Northwest Passage, it's difficult to see why the journey these explorers were attempting was so difficult. The route flows through the bays and channels that lie north of Canada and Alaska. There are lots of islands to navigate around, but why is it so challenging? The answer lies in the extreme cold of the region.

Thousands of giant icebergs, some of which can reach up to 300 feet (90m) in height, drift between Greenland and Baffin Island, forming moving hazards that a captain of a ship might struggle to avoid.

FRIEND OR FOE?

The indigenous people of Canada are mainly Inuit, Algonquians and Iroquois. These natives were living in Canada at the time when European explorers, from the 1500s onwards, started to investigate and attempt to settle these northern lands. Success or failure of a European settlement or expedition was often linked to how well the explorers' meetings with the natives went.

On Frobisher's trips, he had hostile encounters with the local Inuit. Neither group of people trusted each other. On his first trip, five of Frobisher's men disappeared and several Inuit were kidnapped or killed.

This illustration, which was made a only few years after Frobisher's last voyage to the area, shows his men in conflict with the Greenland Inuit.

SURVIVING A WINTER

Expeditions searching for the Northwest Passage would usually expect to have to spend a winter on board their ship, when the sea froze over. The crew would be at risk from cold, hunger and frostbite. If the ship's provisions had not been well planned, the sailors could be at risk of scurvy too. Thomas James, who explored the area in search of the Northwest Passage in 1631, describes the cold on board ship as being

'… so extreme that it was not endurable: no clothes were proof against it: no motion could resist it. It would, moreover, so freeze the hair on our eyelids that we could not see.'

Continuing their voyage and searching for openings they believed led to the Pacific, sailors may have found the way blocked by impassable sea ice. Large chunks of pack ice could smash into their ships and they might encounter 'a very great gulfe' of whirling waters as described by John Davis on his third attempt to find the Northwest Passage in 1587.

If you were the captain of a ship and you managed to avoid your small, wooden vessel being taken out by an iceberg or pack ice, you might have found yourself attempting to sail during the winter months. Very quickly you would have seen the sea around you start to freeze, so a good captain would find a sheltered spot in which to stop for the winter before attempting to continue the voyage.

'IT'S JUST THE TIP OF THE ICEBERG!'

AN ICEBERG CAN BE MASSIVE BUT USUALLY WE CAN ONLY SEE A VERY SMALL PART OF IT, THE TIP, ABOVE THE SEA'S SURFACE. HIDDEN BELOW LIES THE REMAINDER OF THE ICEBERG, WHICH CAN CAUSE PASSING SHIPS BIG PROBLEMS.

The French in Canada

In 1603 Samuel de Champlain was given the task of finding a way across the notoriously tricky Lachine Rapids towards China. He had a skiff, which was a small, open, one-masted boat, designed specifically for the task of navigating the rough water, but it failed. He realised that the relatively simple canoes designed by the indigenous people were actually much better for the job! However, even with this discovery, he didn't find a way through the Canadian interior to China.

LOCAL INUIT SEA CANOES WERE BUILT OF BONE AND DRIFTWOOD. SEALSKIN WAS THEN STRETCHED OVER THE FRAME.

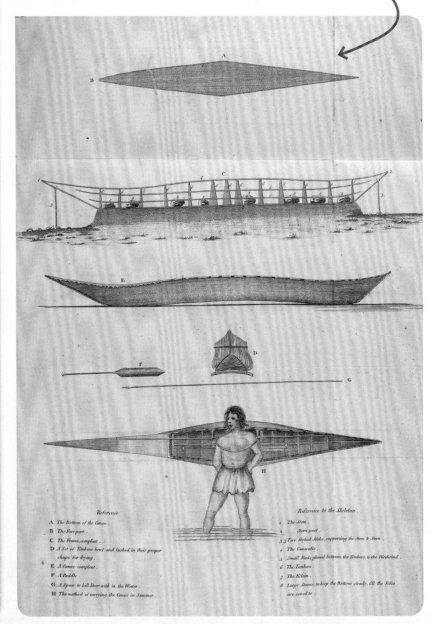

WHAT HAPPENED TO HUDSON?

Henry Hudson has the rare privilege of having not one, not two but three waterways named after him – the Hudson River, the Hudson Strait and the vast Hudson Bay. However it wasn't all good news for him. After discovering Hudson Bay, he spent the winter with his crew waiting for the ice to break up before he could continue his explorations. Sadly for Hudson, his crew, after suffering through a miserable winter, weren't keen to join him, so they put the explorer, his young son and seven other crewmen on a boat and set them adrift. The nine men were never seen again.

Even further north

In 1616 William Baffin and Robert Bylot led an expedition north, battling against sea ice in the Davis Strait to reach the open water of a bay, now called Baffin Bay, beyond. They reached a latitude of 78° north, the furthest north any explorer would go for another 200 years! Though Baffin did not know it at the time, he did actually pass the entrance to the Northwest Passage, Lancaster Sound. Unfortunately for him, it was blocked by sea ice at the time so he wasn't able to explore any further. It was nearly 400 years later that the Northwest Passage would finally be sailed through. Between 1903 and 1906 Roald Amundsen, the famous Norwegian explorer, successfully navigated through the tricky, ice-laden waters in his ship, *Gjøa*.

TAKE THE SHORTCUT

In the 21st century, even with the availability of huge cargo aeroplanes, we still need to sail between Europe and the Far East. There are two routes available to today's enormous container ships. The first is the Panama Canal, which divides the continents of North and South America, linking the Atlantic and the Pacific Oceans. The second is the Suez Canal, which enables ships to travel from the Mediterranean to the Red Sea and, therefore, ultimately connects the Atlantic to the Indian Ocean.

Pirate on the High Seas

Francis Drake led a fleet of ships across the Atlantic in 1577 and returned to England nearly three years later to a hero's welcome. He had a hoard of treasure in the hold, and the glory of being the first ship's captain to circumnavigate the world.

Pirate, adventurer, explorer, commander

Francis Drake's successful life at sea began in Devon, England, when he became an apprentice on ships belonging to the wealthy Hawkins family. Over time John Hawkins had come to the attention of Queen Elizabeth I, as did his most impressive captain, Francis Drake, who had made a name for himself raiding Spanish colonies and ships in Central America.

VOYAGE FACTS

When: December 1577 to September 1580

Where: Around the world

How: He started out with five ships but returned home with only one, the *Golden Hinde*

Why: It's a secret!

Who: Francis Drake

DRAKE RAIDING CARTAGENA, BOLIVIA.

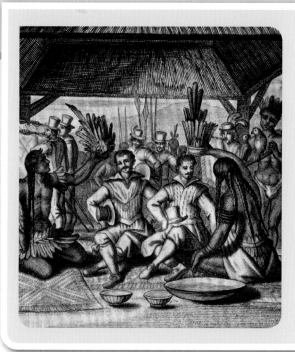

THE SLAVE TRADE

John Hawkins is often known as England's first slave trader. Between 1562 and 1567 Hawkins made three voyages to Guinea and Sierra Leone in Africa and, during this time, it's estimated that around 1,200 Africans were taken as slaves. Drake worked as an apprentice on the Hawkins ships and rose through the ranks to eventually captain a vessel, the *Pinnacle*, on Hawkins' third slaving voyage.

As well as making a lot of money for himself and his family, Hawkins' success was recognised by Queen Elizabeth. Slavery was eventually banned in England in 1772 and outlawed in all British territories in 1833.

A secret mission

The *Pelican*, captained by Francis Drake, led a fleet of five ships across the Atlantic Ocean from Cornwall in 1577. The purpose of this voyage is not really known but it might have been a secret mission set by Queen Elizabeth to anger the Spaniards.

The journey didn't start well. Just a few days after the ships left Plymouth, a storm whipped up at sea and the ships were forced to take shelter in Falmouth where they had to be repaired. Drake wasn't happy and blamed the people who had been loading the ships for their troubles. Eventually they got under way and headed out into the ocean.

Like many voyages across the Atlantic at the time, the ships landed in several places before heading to the Americas. Drake stopped in briefly on the African coast and then at the Cape Verde islands, where he looted the cargo of a Portuguese ship. After spending a few months at sea, the expedition reached the coast of present-day Uruguay in April 1578 and then turned south.

Only three of the five ships arrived in Port St Julian in present-day southern Argentina, where the crew planned to spend the winter before making their way through the notoriously tricky Strait of Magellan. The other two boats had been abandoned.

As the five ships crossed the Atlantic, Drake and Thomas Doughty, possibly his second-in-command, had a big falling out. No one is really sure what the disagreement was about. It may have been because Drake thought that Doughty wanted to lead a mutiny or that he practised a type of magic. Doughty's ship was abandoned because it was in poor condition but Drake believed that Doughty had cursed the ship.

At sea, the captain's word was law. Any hint that there may have been someone stirring up trouble needed to be dealt with swiftly and sternly, before any other crewmembers got the idea that they could turn against the captain. Drake found Doughty guilty of mutiny and conspiracy and sentenced him to death. He was executed at Port St Julian.

And then there was one...

Drake's ship, the *Pelican*, which he renamed the *Golden Hinde*, was the only ship to continue on the voyage after passing through the Strait of Magellan. Just after the three ships had entered the Pacific Ocean, storms blew them apart. The *Golden Hinde* was blown to the southernmost point of South America, the *Marigold* sank with all of its crewmembers and the *Elizabeth* turned sail and headed back to England.

When the *Golden Hinde* was blown off course, Drake made an important discovery. At the time when Drake was sailing, it was assumed there was a large landmass, a southern continent, lying below South America and possibly joined to it. As Drake rounded Cape Horn, the headland of an island that lies below the Strait of Magellan, he saw only ocean and realised there was not another continent joining on to it.

DRAKE'S SHIP, THE *PELICAN* (LATER RENAMED THE *GOLDEN HINDE*).

THIS MAP FROM THE 1590S SHOWS DRAKE'S ROUTE AROUND THE WORLD. CAN YOU SEE THE SHIP *ELIZABETH* ABOUT TO TURN AROUND AT THE TIP OF SOUTH AMERICA?

ON DRAKE'S VOYAGE AROUND THE WORLD, HE AND HIS CREW SAW PENGUINS FOR THE FIRST TIME AND THOUGHT THAT 'IN THEIR HEAD, EYES AND FEET THEY BE LIKE A DUCK BUT ALMOST AS A GOOSE.' DO YOU THINK THAT'S A GOOD DESCRIPTION OF THEM?

Wild winds

Sailing in the waters around South America was not for the faint-hearted. Sailors were a long way from home, facing unfamiliar and sometimes frightening conditions. This description of Drake's voyage through Patagonia by the Reverend Francis Fletcher, who travelled with him, shows just what they had to put up with, and explains how the ships could quite easily have been blown off their course.

'The mountains, being very high and some reaching into the frozen region, did send out their several winds. Sometimes two or three of these winds would come together and meet as if it was one body and violently fall into the sea, whirling that they would pierce into the very bowels of the sea and make it swell upwards on every side.'

Drake the pirate

After the *Golden Hinde* had made it safely through the Strait of Magellan into the Pacific Ocean, it turned north and sailed up the west coast of South America. Drake, ever the pirate, raided Spanish settlements on the way and plundered ships for their treasure. While he was raiding ships in the harbour in Lima, he heard of a Spanish treasure ship called the *Cacafuego* that was said to be full of silver and jewels. Drake chased the ship up the coast towards Panama, where he managed to intercept it and stole hundreds of thousands of pesos worth of silver.

Eventually Drake reached California, past the last of the Spanish settlements. It's possible he even made it as far north as present-day San Francisco. Drake claimed this land for Queen Elizabeth and named it Albion.

SPANISH TREASURE SHIP THE *CACAFUEGO*.

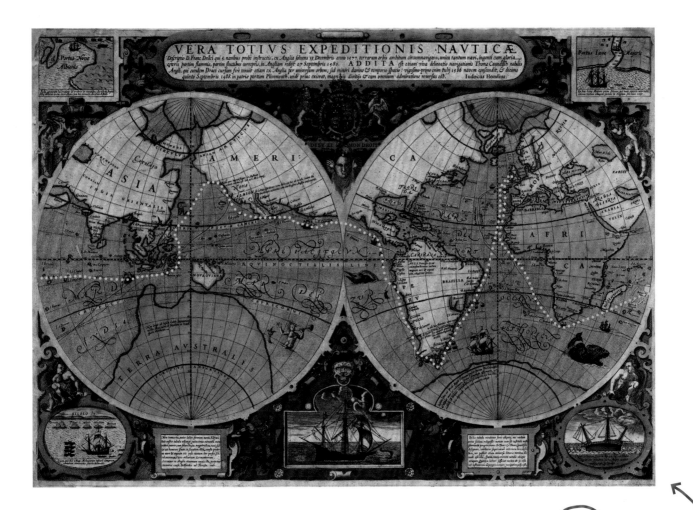

This map, which is sometimes known as Drake's Treasure Map, was drawn by Jodocus Hondius in 1595. The highlighted dots show the route that Drake took to circumnavigate the world, including where he landed in North America. Can you spot Nova Albion on the map, just above California?

DRAKE'S CHECKLIST

Annoy the Spanish ✓

Loot lots of treasure ✓

Gather information about the Pacific Ocean ✓

Be the first ship's captain to circumnavigate the world ✓

DID YOU KNOW?

Drake vs Spain
Francis Drake is also famous for being one of three commanders to defeat the Spanish Armada in 1588 – but that's another story.

Back to Queen and country

In July 1579 Drake left North America and sailed south-west across the Pacific. He passed through the Philippines and the East Indies, rounded the Cape of Good Hope at the tip of Africa, and arrived back in Portsmouth, England, in September 1580. The treasure he brought back was worth around £600,000 at the time, which would be millions of pounds in today's money. Queen Elizabeth was delighted by Drake's return – she loved her treasure and the fact he had angered the Spanish by his pirating. She made Drake a knight just over six months later.

A Pioneering Woman

Maria Sibylla Merian loved painting insects but she was no longer excited by the exotic but dead specimens brought back to Europe by male explorers. She decided that she wanted to voyage to the jungle herself and didn't care that a woman travelling this way was highly unusual.

VOYAGE FACTS

When: 1699–1701

Where: The rainforests of Suriname, South America

How: Sailed across the Atlantic and used axes to hack a way through the rainforest

Why: For science!

Who: Maria Sibylla Merian together with her daughter, Dorothea Maria

Who was Maria Sibylla Merian?

Maria Sibylla Merian was born in Frankfurt, Germany, in 1647. After her father died, her mother remarried the painter Jacob Marell. As Merian grew up, she was inspired by her stepfather and began painting – mainly flowers and insects, especially caterpillars, and became known as an excellent botanical and entomological illustrator. Merian was particularly interested in studying how caterpillars transformed into butterflies.

WHAT IS A BOTANICAL ARTIST?

A botanical artist is someone who draws and paints plants and flowers. Merian was also an entomological illustrator, someone who draws and paints insects. These were very important professions in a world where cameras didn't exist. Artists like Merian were relied upon by the scientific community, and by those with a thirst for knowledge, to produce accurate drawings that truly reflected the wonders of nature – from the smallest of insects to the tallest of trees.

Suriname

AN ENTOMOLOGIST IS A PERSON WHO STUDIES INSECTS.

Goal setting

Merian moved to Holland from Germany with her two daughters when she separated from her husband. She was still interested in caterpillars, and how they became butterflies, but was frustrated that she could only study and paint dead, pinned specimens that had been brought back to Amsterdam by male travellers to Dutch colonies, especially Suriname. Merian wanted to see the living animals for herself. She worked really hard for eight years, proving to local scientists that she was up to the job. Finally, all of her hard work paid off and the City of Amsterdam awarded her a grant to travel to the Dutch colony of Suriname. This was a massive achievement because, at the time, these grants were usually only awarded to men.

A bug-tastic book

In 1705, a couple of years after her return from South America, Merian published *Metamorphosis Insectorum Surinamensium* (*The Metamorphosis of the Insects of Suriname*). It was a groundbreaking book and caused quite a stir in the scientific community.

Unusually for the time, she drew different animals and insects together on the plants upon which they lived. People were used to seeing illustrations of spiders on one page, butterflies on another. Merian drew the creatures as she had seen them in real life, interacting with each other – even if that meant showing them eating each other.

THIS IS HOW MERIAN DESCRIBED BIRD-EATING SPIDERS IN HER BOOK PUBLISHED IN 1705.

'I found many of these large black spiders on the guava trees. They are covered with hair all over and have sharp teeth, with which they can bite fiercely, at the same time injecting a fluid into the wound. When they fail to find enough ants [to eat] they take small birds from their nests and suck all the blood from their bodies.'

A successful trio

Merian set an inspiring example to her two daughters. Johanna Helena, her eldest daughter, moved to Suriname with her husband in 1711. She became a well known artist in her own right, specialising in plants and animals.

Dorothea Maria, the younger daughter who had accompanied her mother on her voyage, went to St Petersburg to work as a scientific illustrator for Peter I, Tsar of Russia. She broke convention by becoming the first woman to be employed by the Russian Academy of Sciences.

THIS DRAWING OF A CAIMAN AND A SNAKE WAS MADE BY DOROTHEA MARIA, MERIAN'S YOUNGER DAUGHTER.

APPEARANCES CAN BE DECEPTIVE

In 1766 Jeanne Baret, a French plant expert, wanted to work on board an explorer's ship but women travelling in this way were still frowned upon. So she and the ship's botanist, Philibert Commerçon, came up with an ingenious plan – she should disguise herself as a boy. Baret managed to keep her secret for many years, wrapping her body in bandages to give herself a more manly shape. It wasn't until the ship docked at the island of Tahiti that Baret's cover was blown. A local saw straight through her disguise and commented to the captain how unusual it was to see a woman on board. The captain was embarrassed and very cross! When Baret arrived back in France she became the first woman to have circumnavigated the globe.

Captain Cook's Voyage of Discovery

Captain James Cook led a voyage to Tahiti in the Southern Ocean to observe our solar system but it was his unexpected discoveries on our own planet that made him a true explorer.

Who was James Cook?

James Cook was born in Scotland in 1728. He began his seafaring career with the merchant navy in Whitby, North Yorkshire. The house where he lived in Whitby is now the Captain Cook Memorial Museum. In 1755 he joined the Royal Navy where he became known for his excellent navigational skills.

VOYAGE FACTS

When: August 1768 to July 1771

Where: Plymouth to the Southern Ocean

How: Aboard a former coalship, the *Endeavour*

Why: In the name of science but there was also a secret challenge

Who: Captain James Cook led a crew of 96 sailors and scientists

Tahiti

Watching Venus

The main reason for Captain Cook's voyage to Tahiti was to watch the planet Venus travel across the sun. Along with 'Officers, Seamen Gentlemen and their servants' he also took two astronomers with him on board his ship, the *Endeavour*, to take measurements of this event. Scientists at the time thought that by finding out how long it took for Venus to pass across the sun, they would be able to work out the distance between Earth and the sun and, from that, even work out the size of the universe!

HOW DID THEY FIND THEIR WAY?

Captain Cook used a marine chronometer, which was a special type of clock used by sailors to tell the time while they were at sea. They used this information to work out how far they had sailed.

The team set sail from Plymouth, England, on 25 August 1768 and arrived in Tahiti just over seven months later. It was a welcome relief to the crew to reach the tropical island after spending two-and-a-half months crossing the Pacific Ocean, often in freezing conditions and braving icy storms.

They spent three months on the island, watching Venus pass across the sun on 3 June 1769 and making detailed notes about Tahiti.

The far south

When Captain Cook and his crew finished their scientific studies in Tahiti, he opened a sealed envelope from King George III that contained secret orders to look for a continent that many people imagined existed in the far south.

INSTRUCTIONS
from His Majesty, King George III

You are to proceed to the southward in order to make discovery of the continent until you arrive in the latitude of 40°.

If you discover the continent you are to employ yourself in exploring as great an extent of the coast as you can.

You are also with the consent of the natives to take possession of convenient situations in the country in the name of the King of Great Britain.

These instructions meant the explorers had to sail to the latitude of 40° south to search for Terra Australis Incognita, which means 'unknown land of the south' in Latin. It was thought that the Southern Continent was a giant landmass of fertile soil with rocks containing precious metals. The effort of finding the land and claiming it for Britain would be well worth it.

Captain Cook set a course southwards, following the instructions. The further south they sailed, the colder it got – so cold that the sailors' fingers would freeze to the rigging!

As they got nearer and nearer to the location that the King had specified, everyone on board was looking out for the continent. You can imagine the excitement as someone shouted out they had seen land, and then the disappointment when they realised that they were only looking at a bank of fog. All the explorers could see was sea, so Captain Cook headed back north and on to the final part of his mission, which was to claim New Zealand for Britain and to map its coastline.

TASMAN'S SHIPS AT ANCHOR IN NEW ZEALAND.

NOT THE FIRST

Dutch sailors first sighted Australia's northwest coast in the early 1600s and Frederik de Houtman made landfall near present-day Perth in 1619, but he didn't go ashore.

Abel Tasman sailed around Australia in 1642 and discovered an island off the south coast, which was later named Tasmania after him.

Australia

Once he'd finished his work in New Zealand, where he confirmed that it was made up of two islands, Captain Cook headed to New Holland, which we now call Australia, to explore its shores. In April 1770 the *Endeavour* dropped anchor in a bay near present-day Sydney. The explorers were so impressed by the large number of new plant specimens that they were able to collect that they named the site Botany Bay.

The whole expedition nearly fell apart when the *Endeavour* crashed into the Great Barrier Reef on its way north. The ship was stranded on the reef for nearly 24 hours before the crew managed to refloat her and Captain Cook used his expertise to carefully sail her up the coast to find somewhere safe to stay while they repaired the damage. The repairs took seven weeks, during which time the crew befriended the local Aboriginal people and checked out the unusual wildlife. The explorers eventually arrived back in Britain, nearly three years after they'd left, in July 1771.

> BOTANY MEANS THE STUDY OF PLANTS.

THIS MAP OF BOTANY BAY WAS DRAWN BY CAPTAIN COOK.

Cook sets sail again

Despite the achievements of his first great voyage, Captain Cook felt that his work in the south seas wasn't complete.

Less than a year after he'd arrived home, Captain Cook received an order to sail further south than anyone had ever been before. This was a challenge that suited the adventurous captain perfectly. In 1773 he finally crossed the Antarctic Circle. He sailed along the edge of the ice shelf and then the whole way around Antarctica. Captain Cook proved that the land he had been searching for, rich, fertile and full of precious rocks, did not exist.

This is how Captain Cook and Captain James King described surfing in Hawaii in their 1784 book *A Voyage to the Pacific Ocean*.

'The men sometimes go without the swell of the surf, and lay themselves flat upon an oval piece of plank about their size and breadth: they keep their legs close on the top of it, and their arms are used to guide the plank. They wait the time for the greatest swell that sets on shore, and altogether push forward with their arms to keep on its top: it sends them in with a most astonishing velocity, and the great art is to guide the plank so as always to keep in a proper direction on the top of the swell.'

Christmas Bay, Antarctica

COOK NAMED THE ISLANDS OF HAWAII THE SANDWICH ISLANDS AFTER HIS SPONSOR, THE EARL OF SANDWICH – NOT AFTER HIS LUNCH!

On his third voyage, which began in July 1776, Captain Cook aimed to find the Northwest Passage that so many previous explorers had failed to find (see pages 34 to 39 for more about this). On his way across the Pacific to North America in his ship, the *Resolution*, Captain Cook and his crew made landfall on the islands of Hawaii. They were the first Europeans to do so and were, therefore, the first Europeans to see Hawaiians surfing.

From Hawaii they headed north, towards the Arctic Ocean, but didn't find a passage to the Atlantic so sailed south again to make their way home. Captain Cook decided to stop at the Hawaiian Islands again and, sadly, that's where his journey ended. He was killed in a fight with some locals in February 1779.

CAPTAIN COOK'S TOP ACHIEVEMENTS

He discovered more of the Earth's surface than any other person.

He made sure that none of his crew died of scurvy by insisting that they ate a proper, balanced diet.

He pioneered the art of scientific navigation with maps. Some of his maps were so accurate they were still being used in the 20th century.

THIS MAP SHOWS THE ROUTES OF ALL THREE OF COOK'S MAJOR VOYAGES.
CAN YOU SPOT NEW HOLLAND AND VAN DIEMAN'S LAND?
YOU'LL KNOW THEM BETTER AS AUSTRALIA AND TASMANIA.

Discovering the Wild West

Meriwether Lewis and William Clark led a team of men, known as the Corps of Discovery, into the American Wild West. Their intention was to find an easy trade route to the Pacific, but along the way they discovered more about the new United States than they ever expected.

The birth of a nation

On 4 July 1776 the Declaration of Independence announced that 13 North American British colonies would separate from Great Britain. Together these 13 colonies became known as the United States.
In 1803 Emperor Napoleon Bonaparte of France sold the Louisiana Territory (which stretched from Montana in the north of America to Louisiana in the south) to the United States, effectively doubling the size of the new country. Thomas Jefferson, the president of the United States, decided that these new lands should be explored and studied for science. At the same time, Americans should try to find a way to reach the Pacific Ocean by boat.

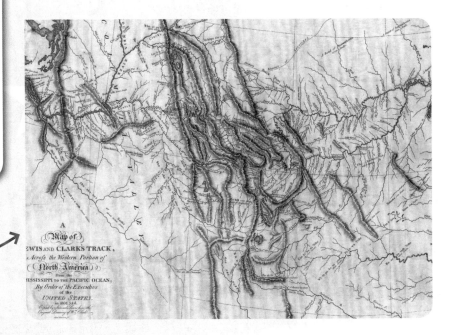

MAP OF LEWIS AND CLARK'S TRACKS.

A HARD-WORKING BOAT

The keelboat Lewis and Clark travelled in had been specially designed for the trip. It was flexible enough to cope with different river conditions and also land that the explorers might have to travel over. It could be sailed, rowed, punted with poles and even pulled across the land. This is a modern replica of the keelboat they used.

WILLIAM CLARK

MERIWETHER LEWIS

Co-Captains

When President Jefferson was choosing who should lead his expedition across America, he didn't feel the need to look any further than his trusted personal secretary, Meriwether Lewis. Lewis decided he needed another pair of hands to help him with this important journey, so he asked his friend, William Clark, to join him as co-captain. Lewis and Clark had served as soldiers together. Clark was an expert rifleman and Lewis had been given scientific training in botany (the study of plants), mineralogy (the study of minerals), navigation and medicine. Together they would make a formidable team.

STILL LOOKING FOR THE NORTHWEST PASSAGE...

More than two hundred years after Martin Frobisher first attempted to find the Northwest Passage (pages 34-39 have the full story), explorers were still searching for a convenient shipping route between the Atlantic and Pacific Oceans. People who traded animal fur wanted an easier way to sell to the markets in the east.

An uphill journey

Lewis and Clark put together a team of 31 men to join them, and called themselves, rather grandly, the Corps of Discovery. After making all their necessary preparations and gathering at the starting point of St Louis, in the state of Missouri, the Corps of Discovery began its journey along the Missouri River in the spring of 1804.

It wasn't an easy start for the expedition. The explorers were heading upriver, against the current, which meant they had to work hard poling and pulling their boats. By the end of the summer, they'd covered approximately 1,553 miles (2,500km). The team set up camp for the winter at Fort Mandan, North Dakota, and made plans for the tricky terrain they would face ahead.

THE MISSOURI RIVER

Teamwork

Lewis and Clark knew they would experience challenges in the wilderness, from the hills, mountains, and the wildlife. They also knew that to have any chance of success, they would need the assistance of the local Native American tribes. To tackle the last problem, Lewis and Clark had a translator, a woman from the Shoshone tribe called Sacagawea, who was able to help them talk to the Shoshone people and navigate through her homeland. She gave birth to a son during the expedition!

LANGUAGE BARRIERS

When you visit a country where the local people speak a different language, how do you communicate with them? Do you try to learn some of their language, use a translator, use some kind of sign language, or do you simply speak your own language slowly and loudly and hope for the best? It can be really tricky trying to have a conversation with people who don't share a language with you. Have you ever wondered how early explorers communicated with native populations in the countries they visited?

Captain Cook described exactly this problem when he arrived in Australia in 1770:

'As we approached the shore they all made off, except two men who seemd resolved to oppose our landing. As soon as I saw this I ordered the boats to lay upon their oars in order to speak to them, but this was to little purpose, for neither us nor Tupia could understand one word they said.'

> DO YOU THINK THE *CORPS OF DISCOVERY* IS GOOD NAME FOR A GROUP OF PEOPLE ON AN EXPEDITION TO NEW LANDS? IF YOU WERE LEADING AN EXPEDITION, WHAT WOULD YOU CALL YOURSELVES?

Lewis and Clark arranged a meeting with members of the Oto and Missouri tribes before they even set off on their travels. One reason for this meeting was to teach Lewis and Clark how to appear friendly when making their first contact with tribes they might meet on their travels. They learnt how to make a sign indicating that they were friendly, and the word for 'white man', which was *ta-ba-bone*. Lewis and Clark also bought lots of items to present to the Indians as gifts, as this list shows.

Lewis and Clark on the Columbia River, nearing the end of their journey. In the background are Sacagawea with her baby and husband.

> THE CORPS OF DISCOVERY TRAVELLED A TOTAL OF 8,000 MILES (13,000KM). THEY SUCCESSFULLY FOUND A ROUTE TO THE PACIFIC AND, ALONG THE WAY, DESCRIBED SCIENTIFICALLY FOR THE FIRST TIME MORE THAN 100 NEW SPECIES OF ANIMAL.

WHAT'S IN A NAME?

A fish, commonly known as the 'cutthroat trout' was named *Oncorhynchus clarki* after William Clark, who made a drawing of it.

The Wild West

In the spring of 1805 the explorers left their winter camp and entered the Wild West. The country west of Fort Mandan wasn't empty of people as you might imagine. In fact, Lewis and Clark found it remarkably busy! Native American tribes lived in the area and controlled the land, British and French traders from Canada and Spanish traders from Mexico were all travelling and working there, and then there were the bears! The expedition saw at least 62 grizzly bears on its travels but, according to Clark, it was the 'Musquiters' (mosquitoes) that were very 'troublesome'.

Between the Corps of Discovery and the Pacific Ocean lay a treacherous route across the Bitterroot Range of the Rocky Mountains. They would not be able to get across simply on foot or by boat so Lewis and Clark decided to use horses to help them on the mountain passes. With the help of their translator, Sacagawea, they bought horses from the Shoshone people, who also helpfully provided a guide who knew the land ahead. All of their careful preparation was useless, however, when heavy snow fell, trapping the expedition in the mountains. The travellers ran out of food and had to eat the horses.

Eventually they managed to push on through, built some dugout canoes and shot the rapids down the Clearwater, Snake and Columbia rivers.

'Ocian in view! O! the joy!'

wrote Clark in his journal on 7 November 1805. They had made it to their destination.

BEWARE THE BEARS

This is an illustration by Patrick Gass taken from a journal of the expedition.

During the expedition Lewis was chased by a bear:
"… as soon as he turned, the bear ran open-mouthed and at full speed upon him. Captain Lewis ran about eighty yards, but finding that the animal gained on him fast, he turned short, plunged into the river about waist-deep, and facing about presented the point of his espontoon." An espontoon is a type of pole with a spike fixed to the end.

If you ever plan to go hiking in the wilderness of North America, you'll need to know what to do in case you come across a bear. So here are some handy tips.

- Talk calmly to the bear so that it knows you're human.

- Stay calm.

- Make yourself look as large as possible – you could do this by moving to higher ground.

- If the bear is standing still, move away slowly and sideways – moving sideways is non-threatening to bears.

The Voyage of the Beagle

In 1831 a young naturalist joined a voyage to South America. The discoveries that he made there would change the way the world thought forever.

Paving the way

During the 18th and 19th centuries it became more and more popular to travel for science. Ship's captains led expeditions to make maps of newly found lands and, alongside that, take note of the animals and plants they saw too. It became normal for a ship to have a botanist or a naturalist on board, as well as navigators and surveyors.

These naturalists would busy themselves with collecting plants and animals and then set about describing them scientifically. Excitingly, they were making new discoveries all the time. Some of the botanists and naturalists who made these early voyages gathered vast collections of new species. Philibert de Commerson, a French botantist, collected around 3,000 new species on a three-year voyage around the world between 1766 and 1769 with explorer Louis de Bougainville.

VOYAGE FACTS

When: 27 December 1831 to 2 December 1836

Where: Around the world from Plymouth, England, via South America's west and east coasts, Galapagos Islands, Tahiti, New Zealand, Australia and South Africa

How: On board the *Beagle* – a warship that had been adapted for the voyage

Why: Darwin joined Captain FitzRoy as a companion on a trip originally planned as a two-year survey of the coasts of South America

Who: Charles Darwin, Captain Robert FitzRoy and the crew of the *Beagle*

THE *BEAGLE* IN THE STRAIT OF MAGELLAN AT MONTE SARMIENTO.

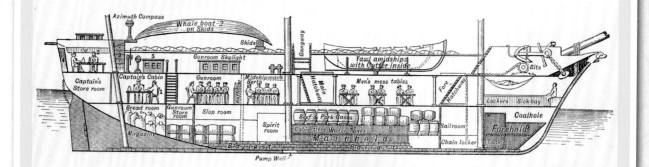

HMS BEAGLE

The *Beagle* started life as a Royal Navy ship, a ten-gun brig sloop. She was refitted to carry out surveys and, under Captain Robert FitzRoy, successfully completed three major voyages. On these voyages, instead of guns, she carried scientific equipment – theodolites, chronometers, barometers. A Beaufort wind scale was used for the first time on her second voyage when Darwin was a passenger.

Alfred Russel Wallace was an English naturalist who spent eight years exploring the Malay Archipelago between 1854 and 1862. He collected more than 125,000 specimens and developed a theory about how animals evolved, which was very similar to the one that Darwin was working on back in England.

ALFRED RUSSEL WALLACE

It wasn't just botanists and naturalists who were exploring the world. Scientists with broader interests were also travelling and making new discoveries. One of these scientific explorers was Alexander von Humboldt, a young German student who had a passion for finding out everything about everything! He travelled to South America in 1799 and studied volcanoes – how they worked and the plants and animals that lived on them. Darwin was a big fan of Humbolt's books, and called him 'the greatest scientific traveller who ever lived'.

ALEXANDER VON HUMBOLDT

Land ahoy!

The voyage to South America was only meant to last two years but it was five years later that the *Beagle* returned to British shores. During those five years, Darwin only spent 533 days on board the ship (that's less than a year and a half). He suffered from seasickness, and took opportunities whenever possible to explore inland while Captain FitzRoy and the *Beagle* sailed up and down surveying the coastline from the water. During Darwin's inland adventures he made observations of the plants and animals he saw there, and collected as many specimens as possible.

We know that Darwin didn't enjoy travelling at sea because he wrote about it:

'...when the water was rough, I was often a little sea-sick; it is no trifling evil, cured in a week.'

WHO WAS CHARLES DARWIN?

When Charles Darwin was growing up in rural England, he loved collecting all sorts of bits and bobs from the world around him such as plants, minerals and shells. As a young adult, he studied to be a clergyman but never lost his love of nature. So when he was offered a place on HMS *Beagle* as a companion to Captain FitzRoy, he jumped at the chance and happily left his clerical studies to join the voyage across the Atlantic Ocean. Darwin was only 22 and FitzRoy only 26 when they set sail from Plymouth in December 1831.

CAPTAIN ROBERT FITZROY

This map shows the approximate route taken by the *Beagle* around South America. Darwin enjoyed making treks on land while the ship sailed along the coast.

ON THE VOYAGE, DARWIN...

Saw tropical rainforest for the first time on the Cape Verde islands.

Took part in the carnival in Rio de Janeiro, Brazil.

Helped to save the expedition from disaster when a wall of ice fell into the water near their survey boats close to Tierra del Fuego at the tip of South America.

Trekked 700 miles (1,125km) in Argentina.

Saw the eruption of volcano Mount Osorno in Chile.

Experienced an earthquake near Valdivia, Chile.

Saw giant tortoises on the Galapagos Islands.

Enjoyed meeting the locals in Tahiti.

Was unimpressed by New Zealand.

Enjoyed the climate in Australia, which he described as 'splendid'.

Trekked through eucalyptus trees to the top of Mount Wellington, Tasmania.

Saw monstrous crabs on the Cocos Islands in the Indian Ocean.

And finally arrived in Falmouth, England, on 2nd December 1836.

Thinking time

When Charles Darwin began his voyage as a young naturalist, he had no idea that what he saw in those far-flung places would lead him to become one of the most famous scientists of all time. From on board his ship, and on his many inland treks, he saw lots of animals that got him thinking.

DARWIN'S FROG

He discovered a small frog while trekking in South America. This frog is unusual because the male carries eggs, which are about to hatch, around in a special pouch until the young are ready to look after themselves. It's called *Rhinoderma darwinii* (Darwin's frog).

GIANT TORTOISES

One of the most remarkable animals Darwin saw on his travels were the giant tortoises that lived on the Galapagos Islands. He noticed that the shape and style of the shell of these tortoises was different on each island.

The tortoises were important to the local people, for whom tortoise meat was a staple part of their diet. When he was on James Island, Darwin ate some too and noted that 'the young tortoises make excellent soup.'

THE GALAPAGOS FINCHES

When Darwin was on the Galapagos Islands, off the coast of Ecuador, he noticed differences between the finches that he saw on each island – though they looked very similar, he spotted that they had slightly different beaks. Darwin collected 14 specimens of finches with different beaks to study further. He worked out that their beaks were suited to eating different types of food, and knew that each Galapagos Island offered a different variety of food. Putting all of this together helped him to develop his famous Theory of Evolution.

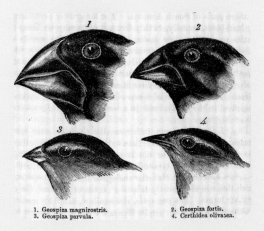

1. Geospiza magnirostris.
2. Geospiza fortis.
3. Geospiza parvula.
4. Certhidea olivasea.

Darwin's Theory of Evolution wasn't actually developed during the voyage. He took very detailed travel notes while he was away and published these, calling them *The Voyage of the Beagle*, shortly after he arrived back in England. Darwin then spent the next few years studying the specimens he and FitzRoy had collected, talking to other scientists, developing his theory and writing his book. *On the Origin of Species by Means of Natural Selection* was finally published in 1859, 28 years after Darwin had set off on his voyage as a young man.

Collecting

To collect the animals to be studied, they had to be killed and then preserved. Darwin collected so many specimens on his travels that there wasn't enough room for them on board the *Beagle* so he had to arrange for them to be sent back to England. Some of these specimens still survive in the Natural History Museum's archives.

Do you like collecting shells when you go to the seaside? Darwin did too. The shells in this specimen drawer stored at the Natural History Museum in London were collected by him as he sailed around the world.

THESE JARS CONTAIN SPECIMENS OF SMALL LIZARDS COLLECTED BY DARWIN DURING HIS VOYAGE.

Into Africa

Dr David Livingstone braved swamps, thick forests, ferocious wild animals and hostile tribes as he explored Africa's interior.

VOYAGE FACTS

When: November 1853 to May 1856

Where: Cape Town to Luanda, then along the Zambezi River to Qualimane

How: On foot and by canoe

Why: Livingstone was looking for somewhere free from disease to found a new mission station and to open up Africa's interior to trade

Who: David Livingstone, along with local porters

A life's mission

David Livingstone decided he wanted to become a medical missionary while he was studying medicine in Glasgow. He applied to join the London Missionary Society, whose aim was to spread Christianity to other countries. His application was successful and he left Britain for southern Africa in 1840 on his very first assignment.

Missionary: *A missionary is someone who wants to spread the word about their own particular religion. Their aim is to convince other people to follow that religion.*

Livingstone's Mission, Kwirara

On his arrival in southern Africa, Livingstone first went to join Robert Moffat's mission station at Kuruman (in the north of today's South Africa) then, together with Roger Edwards, he set out on a journey to look for a location for a new mission. Southern Africa was, and still is today, home to beautiful but dangerous wild animals.

Today it's possible to see these animals in a relatively safe way – on safari with an experienced and knowledgeable guide. In the mid-1800s, when Livingstone began his exploration of Africa's interior, he had to live by his wits and learn to protect himself. Soon after he and Edwards had founded a mission at Mabotse, Livingstone was attacked by a lion.

'I saw the lion just in the act of springing upon me; he caught my shoulder as he sprang, and we both came to the ground below together. Growling horribly close to my ear, he shook me as a terrier dog does a rat.'

Livingstone was saved from this attack by his companions, who shot and speared the lion. The lion died from its injuries. Livingstone's shoulder bone was 'crushed into splinters', and he had 'eleven teeth wounds' on his arm.

Coast to coast

Livingstone's children and his wife, Mary, were living in England when he began his most famous journey. In November 1853 he walked north from Cape Town, through the Kalahari Desert to Lake Ngami. He then turned west, into unfamiliar territory full of potential danger, with an aim to reach Luanda on Africa's west coast. Livingstone travelled with 27 men that his friend, Chief Sekeletu, had lent him. They struggled through swamps in heavy rain, keeping a wary eye out for hostile tribes. Thick forest threatened to block their way, food was scarce, they ran out of things to trade and they got very ill. After six months of tough travel, the expedition finally reached the coast. Livingstone collapsed from hunger and illness. He was offered a boat back to England but refused it, choosing instead to stay with his men and return east, back the way they had come.

FAMILY TRAVELS

David Livingstone met his wife, Mary, while he was recovering from his lion-inflicted injuries. She was the daughter of Robert Moffat, who ran the mission at Kuruman where Livingstone recuperated. She had been born in Africa and spoke Setswana, the language of the local people. Together they founded their own mission in 1847 at Kolobeng in the south of present-day Botswana.

While they were living there, Livingstone's career as an explorer began. He trekked across the Kalahari Desert with three friends and then set his sights on the Zambezi River. One of the reasons for this trek was to find a site for a new mission. They were looking for somewhere that would be free from mosquitos, biting flies that cause the disease malaria, and tsetse flies, which killed livestock. Mary and their young children joined him on this expedition, risking their lives not only from the carnivorous wild animals that roamed the land but also from fever caused by malaria. Mary sadly died from the disease in 1863 on an expedition on the River Zambezi.

This drawing of Livingstone's family on the shores of Lake Ngami is from his book, *Missionary Travels*.

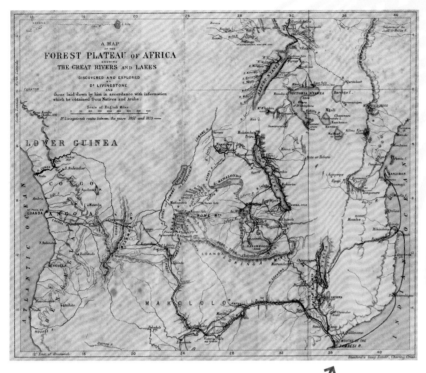

The red lines on this map mark out the many routes travelled by Livingstone on his exploration of Africa

"SMOKE THAT THUNDERS"

After travelling west for about 50 miles (80km) down the Zambezi River, Livingstone saw columns of 'smoke' rising in the distance. This was the water vapour rising up through the air from the spectacular waterfalls, which he named Victoria Falls. He was the first European to see them. The local name for them was *Mosiotunya* or 'smoke that thunders'.

They reached Shesheke, which Livingstone had passed through on his way up from Cape Town, and decided to continue to try to reach Africa's east coast by sailing down the Zambezi River. He was given more men by Chief Sekeletu and fresh supplies. The journey east was just as tough as the journey west had been. Hungry crocodiles, angry hippos and spear-wielding local tribes were daily hazards for the men, as well as bad weather and lack of food.

THIS CANOE WAS UNLUCKY ENOUGH TO BE CAPSIZED BY AN ANGRY HIPPOPOTAMUS!

More than five months after passing by Victoria Falls, Livingstone's long journey finally came to an end. In May 1856 he reached Quilimane on the east coast of present-day Mozambique, and returned to England to a hero's welcome and a gold medal from the Royal Geographical Society.

Search for the source

The River Nile, which flows through north-east Africa into the Mediterranean Sea, is the world's longest river. It is formed from two rivers, the Blue Nile and the White Nile. For many years, explorers had searched for the source of the Nile rivers, the place where the water first flows and starts its long journey towards the sea. In 1618 the Spaniard Pedro Páez discovered the source of the Blue Nile in Ethiopia but the source of the White Nile remained unknown.

In the 1850s the Royal Geographical Society decided to launch an expedition to search for the source of the White Nile. Richard Burton and John Hanning Speke led the quest. They reached Lake Tanganyika, which they thought could have been the source, but on seeing it they realised they were wrong. By this time, Burton was too ill to continue so Speke carried on without him. He reached another lake, which he then claimed was the source of the Nile, and named it Lake Victoria.

JOHN HANNING SPEKE

MAP OF SPEKE'S EXPEDITION.

ON A WILD AFRICAN ADVENTURE, WATCH OUT FOR...

LIONS

HIPPOPOTAMUSES

CROCODILES

MOSQUITOES

However another river, called the Kagera River, flowed into Lake Victoria, so surely this needed to be explored to see if it would lead to the source of the White Nile? Speke returned home and the true source of the Nile remained a mystery.

In January 1866 Livingstone was sent by the Royal Geographical Society to make an attempt to find the source of the Nile. Livingstone was happy to go on this expedition as he'd wanted to look for the source for many years. He headed west of Lake Tanganyika to explore but six long years went by and nobody heard from him. Livingstone had been lost!

Journalist Henry Morton Stanley was sent by the Royal Geographical Society to find Livingstone. On 10 November 1871 Stanley saw a tall figure on the shores of Lake Tanganyika, and greeted him with these words:

'Dr Livingstone, I presume.'

Livingstone was coming to the end of his life as an explorer (he died two years later, still in Africa). Stanley was just beginning his adventures on the African continent.

The Desert Queen

Passionate about archaeology and Arab people, Gertrude Bell led a life of adventure and discovery.

Who was Gertrude Bell?

Scholar, traveller, archaeologist, mountaineer, diplomat – Gertrude Bell was all of these things. She studied at Oxford University and became the first woman to be awarded a first-class degree in history. Her life of travelling began in 1892 when she went to Iran with her Aunt Mary to visit her uncle, the British ambassador. Bell was bitten by the travel bug and completed two round-the-world journeys by steamship, climbed the Matterhorn in Switzerland (surviving 53 hours on a rope in a blizzard), visited Jerusalem and Turkey and crossed the Syrian desert!

Bell loved travel for its own sake – and particularly enjoyed journeying around Arabia – but many of her trips focused on her passion for archaeology. In Syria, Turkey and Mesopotamia she excavated medieval and Roman ruins.

VOYAGE FACTS

When: 136 days from December 1913 to April 1914

Where: More than 1,430 miles (2,300km) through the Arabian Desert in the Middle East

How: Camel train

Why: Exploration and discovery

Who: Gertrude Bell

Bell explored the ancient monuments of Syria in 1905 and wrote about her experiences in a book, *The Desert and the Sown*.

> THE WORD *ARCHAEOLOGY* COMES FROM THE GREEK FOR 'THE STUDY OF ANCIENT THINGS'

A group of camels, such as the seventeen that accompanied Bell on her trek, is usually known as a camel train or a caravan. Here her camels are having a well earned drink.

A desert trek

Between December 1913 and April 1914, Bell travelled across the desert. She left the city of Damascus in Syria with the aim of visiting Hail, where no European had set foot for twenty years because it was considered unsafe. She faced hostility from local desert tribes, which had a history of being violent to members of other tribes and foreigners, especially the British. On this trip, Bell entered one of the most dangerous environments on Earth. The sun beat down relentlessly, sandstorms could whip up at a moment's notice and there was the risk she might not find water for days.

Mesopotamia means 'between two rivers'. It refers to the land between the rivers Euphrates and Tigris. Most of Mesopotamia lies in modern-day Iraq.

Prepared for the worst

Bell's experience of travelling across deserts and through Arabia helped her prepare for this trek. She knew that to survive many days in the desert, she would need enough food and water to last the long distances between desert oases, a guide, some servants and plenty of camels (she had seventeen for this journey) to carry everything.

Bell's time spent learning Arabic, as well as the languages and customs of the desert tribes she was likely to meet, helped her during her journey. She was able to charm some of the local sheikhs, who then ensured she would have safe passage through tribal-run areas. Bell brought gifts with her to present to tribal leaders and hoped that, as a woman, she would pose less threat to them than a British man would have done. Despite her careful preparation, Bell still encountered problems on her journey. One group of mountain tribesmen threatened Bell's group with a rifle and stole many of their possessions, including their guns and cloaks. Luckily for Bell, before things got too bad, one of them recognised her camel herder and they stopped their attack.

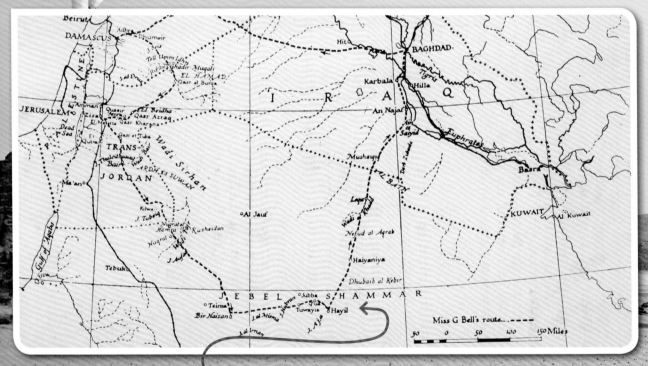

Place names can often be spelt in a number of different ways. On this map, which shows the route of Bell's desert trek, Hail is shown as Hayil, though it could also be spelt Ha'il or even Ha'yel.

Please may I come in?

After the attack, Bell and her team continued on their desert trek for two months before they reached the town of Hail. No European had been able to enter the city walls for more than twenty years, but Bell was welcomed in. She was allowed in the palace and given food and company but, unfortunately, she was then not allowed to leave, and was kept prisoner for eleven days. Eventually she was set free and went on her way to Baghdad and then back to Damascus.

The Royal Geographical Society awarded Bell a Gold Medal for her journey to Hail. She then began a new chapter in her life.

HAIL, WHERE BELL WAS IMPRISONED FOR MORE THAN A WEEK.

On 23 January 1914, Gertrude Bell wrote in a letter:

'We have marched for two days across exceedingly featureless country... It is a desolate land – barren beyond all belief.'

CAMEL FACTS

- Camels are able to cope with extreme temperatures – both hot and cold – which is lucky because deserts can get very cold at night.

- They can survive for many weeks without water.

- Camel hair can be used to make clothes.

- Camels with one hump, like those found in Arabia, are called dromedaries.

- Those with two humps are called Bactrian camels.

- It's easy to remember to difference – two humps looks like a sideways letter B, and one hump looks like a sideways D!

A spy in the sand

On her travels, Bell noted the different political beliefs of the various tribes she encountered, and how they felt about the British. The British government realised that she had gathered a great deal of useful knowledge and decided to put her to work. She became a member of the Arab Bureau, based in Cairo, Egypt, in November 1915. This was during the first world war, when not only Europe but also the Middle East was a place of great tension. Bell provided assistance to the British Forces in Egypt and, after the war, helped to map out the boundaries that form the borders of present-day Iraq, Kuwait and Saudi Arabia.

Gertrude Bell's legacy

Bell was passionate about archaeology. Many of the places she chose to visit were ones of archaeological interest to her. One of her most important digs was an attempt to excavate the ruins of the ancient city of Babylon in present-day Iraq. Bell helped to found Baghdad Archaeological Museum, now known as the Iraq Museum, in 1926. Iraq has suffered many conflicts in modern history, including the Gulf War in 1991. The museum has been closed for much of the past twenty-five years and has had many of its valuable collections looted.

LADY ANNE BLUNT

A painting by Lady Anne Blunt of the pilgrimage to Nejd in present-day Saudi Arabia, which took place between December 1878 and February 1879.

FREYA STARK

ISABELLA BIRD

DERVLA MURPHY

Blazing a trail

Twenty years before Gertrude Bell set out on her journey to Hail, another female explorer, Mary Kingsley, made two trail-blazing trips to west Africa. On her first voyage in 1893, she explored the coast of west Africa, from Sierra Leone to Angola. She also travelled inland and collected animal and plant specimens from the Congo River.

In December 1894 Kingsley returned to Africa, this time with a plan to meet the notoriously fierce Fang tribe. To find these people she would have to travel up the Ogooué River in Gabon by canoe. Even the crocodiles that lived in the waters there did not faze Kingsley. When one made an attempt to climb on to her canoe, she apparently rapped it on the nose with her umbrella.

Kingsley wore her usual style of dress when she travelled. For a Victorian lady that meant petticoats, stiff skirts and a corset. This must have been extremely uncomfortable in the jungle. However, such clothes had advantages. Her thick woollen outfit and many petticoats once saved Kingsley from being impaled by the spikes of a hidden mantrap!

Kingsley returned home in 1895 and wrote a bestselling book about everything she had seen and done, called *Travels in West Africa*.

The Imperial Trans-Antarctic Expedition

It is said that Ernest Shackleton placed this advert in a newspaper for the job of crewmember on his Trans-Antarctic Expedition. Would you have been one of the 5,000 applicants?

The lure of the South Pole...

In 1902 Robert Falcon Scott, Ernest Shackleton and doctor Edward Wilson travelled 400 miles (645km) across the frozen Ross Sea ice shelf.

Between 1907 and 1909 Shackleton led the *Nimrod* expedition, in which he and a team of four men attempted to reach the South Pole. Low supplies forced the explorers to turn back when they were 97 miles (156km) away from their goal.

VOYAGE FACTS

When: 1914–1916

Where: From Plymouth to Antarctica

How: In the *Endurance* and later the *James Caird*

Why: To cross the Antarctic continent

Who: Ernest Shackleton and a crew of twenty-seven men

SCOTT'S DOOMED EXPEDITION.

In December 1911 Scott made it to the South Pole, just days after Norwegian Arctic traveller Roald Amundsen had reached it. Sadly, none of the five men in Scott's expedition to reach the Pole made it back alive.

Who was Ernest Shackleton?

Shackleton learnt his skills as a sailor in his job as a master mariner. A master mariner is someone who is qualified to be a captain of a ship, especially a merchant ship that trades goods between countries. He first experienced Antarctica in 1901, when he joined Scott on the National Antarctic Expedition as third officer. On the Imperial Trans-Antarctic Expedition, Shackleton's crew members called him 'the Boss'.

Bold intentions

The Imperial Trans-Antarctic Expedition, led by Shackleton, hoped to cross the Antarctic continent. It was the next big polar challenge after Amundsen and Scott had reached the South Pole in December 1911. There was glory to be had if Shackleton's team succeeded, but its main focus was to collect data for scientific study.

THE *ENDURANCE* IN THE ICE ON ANTARCTICA.

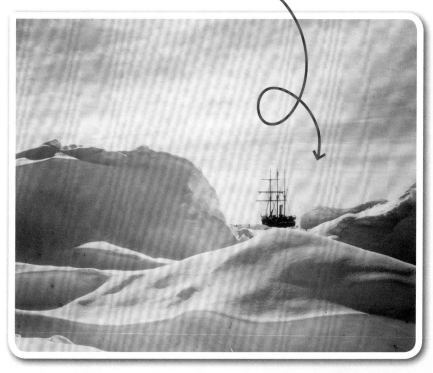

SCIENCE AND THE SOUTH POLE

Locked away in Antarctica's ice are secrets about planet Earth. Scientists study the ice as well as the ocean and rocks to discover more about how the Earth and even the universe were formed. Information taken from the ice can help scientists learn more about climate change. They also look to the skies. Taking advantage of a dry, cold and stable atmosphere with no light pollution, astronomers study the stars and planets.

This is the British Antarctic Survey's Halley VI Research Station. Did you know it can be moved on special skis? It stands on an ice shelf, which flows slowly out into the Weddell Sea, and is at risk from large cracks forming in the ice. In 2017 it was moved 15 miles (25km) upstream.

Due south

Sailing in *Endurance* under Shackleton as captain, the expedition of twenty-eight men left Plymouth on 8 August 1914 and travelled south for nearly three months. The team reached South Georgia at the end of October and prepared for the next stage of the expedition. On 5 December 1914 everything was ready and *Endurance* set sail for Antarctica. Just over two days later they entered pack ice.

After nearly six weeks of steady sailing through the tricky pack ice, the temperature dropped, the ice closed in around the ship and trapped it. *Endurance* was stuck, drifting with the ice, for ten months. The crew spent much of this time on the ship but noticed that the ice was putting pressure on it. The ship was creaking and starting to split.

In November 1915 the crewmembers and their dogs watched helplessly as *Endurance* sank.

If you ever find yourself sailing in pack ice, try to remember these tips:

- Keep your ship moving at all times, even if it's very slowly.

- Don't let your ship move too fast – ice can cause damage if hit at speed.

- Know your ship well – understand how it moves.

- Work with the movement of the ice, try not to battle against it.

THE COLDEST TEMPERATURE EVER RECORDED, -89°C, WAS AT VOSTOCK, A REMOTE ANTARCTIC STATION.

> 'The roar of pressure could be heard all around us. I could hear the creaking and groaning of her timbers, and the faint indefinable whispers of our ship's distress.'

Ernest Shackleton, *South, The Endurance Expedition*

The men were forced to abandon the ship and take with them what they could. They weren't able to save everything – all of the specimens collected by the ship's biologist, Robert Clark, were left on board – but they did manage to save the dogs, most of their provisions and essential equipment, and three lifeboats. The team made camp on the ice and watched as *Endurance* was slowly crushed and then sank beneath the ice on 21 November 1915.

Shackleton chose to save his diary from the sinking ship but he ripped out lots of pages to reduce its weight. What would you save if you could only take a small bag of your possessions?

Losing hope

Drifting on a frozen sea, thousands of miles from home, with no way to communicate with anyone and with no obvious means of escape, the crew of the sunken *Endurance* must have had little hope of survival. Luckily for them, Shackleton was not the kind of person to give up. He knew of supplies at Paulet Island, which was relatively nearby, so he made a plan to make their way there. The team started by marching on the ice and pulling with them two of the lifeboats that they had rescued from the sinking ship. In early April, when the ice started to break up, they got into the boats and set off by sea. Unfortunately they found that there was too much ice in the direction of Paulet Island, so they headed to Elephant Island instead, reaching it in a couple of weeks.

After months of living on floating ice and in boats, they were finally on solid land, but there was still no hope of rescue.

ANTARCTIC FACTS

Antarctica is:

A vast frozen continent and one of most remote places on Earth.

The coldest, driest and windiest continent.

Home to about five million penguins.

THE MOMENT THE *JAMES CAIRD* WAS LAUNCHED.

PENGUIN BURGERS ANYONE?

The men who were left stranded on Elephant Island needed to top up their food stores with fresh meat but they couldn't pop to the local shop to buy a steak. Instead, they hunted penguins and seals – even large elephant seals – and ate those.

The rescue mission

Shackleton decided to take action. He planned to make the perilous journey to South Georgia, where he knew there was a Norwegian whaling station that offered hope of rescue. However, between Shackleton and his destination lay 870 miles (1,400km) of the world's coldest and roughest ocean, and he only had an open, wooden lifeboat, named the *James Caird*, to sail in. It was a desperate situation. Shackleton thought this would be the only way of saving his men from certain death so, on 24 April 1916, six members of the *Endurance* crew set sail.

The twenty-two men who had been left behind almost certainly thought they would never see the six again, and the crew on board the *James Caird* probably thought the same. However, they all knew that they had to give Shackleton's plan a try.

Achieving the impossible

The crew of the *James Caird* spent just over two weeks at sea, being battered by mountainous waves and suffering from extreme cold. They finally landed on South Georgia, but the whaling station and any chance of help was on the other side of the island. In their way were icy mountains to cross. The men rested to recover from their difficult sea journey and, after a couple of days, Shackleton and two others, Worsley and Crean, set out across the mountains. A day-and-a-half later the exhausted men arrived at the whaling station and were finally able to raise the alarm. The remaining crew on Elephant Island were finally rescued on 30 August 1916.

HOW DID THEY FIND THEIR WAY?

The weather at sea was mostly cloudy, which meant the men couldn't rely on 'sun-sights' and their traditional navigating instruments, such as a chronometer, sextant and compass, to help them plot their route. Instead the ship's navigator, Worsley, used old seafaring tricks – such as watching the waves and feeling the wind on the back of his neck – to work out the direction of travel.

EXTREME SURVIVAL

The crew of the *James Caird* faced enormous waves and freezing temperatures. Their clothes didn't help, either. Their oilskins, perfectly designed for wet conditions, had been abandoned with the sinking *Endurance* and they were left with thick wool layers. Sea spray made these wet and they froze, causing painful blisters, chapped skin and frostbite. To warm up, they attempted to make themselves hot drinks using a small camping stove. Imagine trying to get that to work on a swaying boat!

To the Moon

On 16 July 1969 three brave men began a voyage that they hoped would make history. Their destination was the Moon.

VOYAGE FACTS

When: 16–24 July 1969

Where: From Kennedy Space Center, Florida, USA to the Moon and back

How: *Saturn V* rocket and *Eagle* lunar module

Why: The space race

Who: Neil Armstrong, Buzz Aldrin and Michael Collins

The space race

By the middle of the 20th century humans had reached both the North and the South Poles, crossed vast oceans, trekked through impenetrable jungles and climbed the highest mountains. Where next? Why, space of course!

In the 1950s the USA and the Soviet Union were competing with each other to develop the best and safest rockets in which to send humans into space and, most importantly, get them home again. The Soviet Union won the first challenge, when it successfully sent Yuri Gagarin on an orbit around Earth on 12 April 1961 in *Vostock 1*. He travelled 190 miles (300km) above Earth and circled it once before returning.

The USA felt under pressure to make the next big leap in the space race – and what could be more dramatic and world-changing than landing humans on the Moon? The National Aeronautics and Space Administration (NASA) launched the *Gemini* programme in 1961. This was a series of space flights, including space walks and and docking exercises, where one spacecraft would link up with another. What the Americans learnt from the Gemini spaceflight programme would be used in the the Apollo missions, which aimed to put NASA astronauts on the Moon.

In 1961 Yuri Gagarin became the first man to orbit the Earth.

Blast off!

On 16 July 1969 the countdown clock finally reached 00:00:00 and the *Saturn V* rocket blasted off from Kennedy Space Centre in Florida, carrying Mission Commander Neil Armstrong, Buzz Aldrin and Michael Collins on a journey into space. Within eleven minutes they had left Earth's atmosphere and were already weightless. The men then faced a three-day journey before they got close to the Moon.

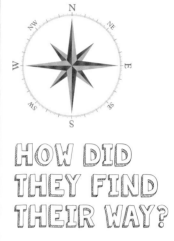

HOW DID THEY FIND THEIR WAY?

The route to the Moon was programmed into *Saturn V*'s onboard computer. Back on Earth, at Mission Control in Houston, ground-tracking systems could send information to the onboard computer.

HOW WOULD IT FEEL TO BE BLASTED INTO SPACE?

Saturn V was 363 feet (111m) tall – that's bigger than the Statue of Liberty! It was cleverly designed in three separate stages, each with its own engine and fuel supply. As each stage emptied its fuel tank, it would be jettisoned away and the rest of the rocket would continue onwards. Most of the energy generated by the engines was used to push the rocket into Earth's orbit. The last burst of energy was used to propel the rocket towards the Moon. The first two stages splashed down into the ocean once they were separated from the rocket. No one knows what happened to the final stage – it might have hit the Moon, or perhaps it's still floating around in space.

Lunar landing

On day four of their journey, the astronauts passed by the 'dark side' of the Moon – that's the side of the Moon we can't see from Earth. At this point they were orbiting 62 miles (100km) above the surface of the Moon. Armstrong and Aldrin now transferred from the command module, known as *Columbia*, into the lunar module, known as *Eagle*, and on 20 July 1969 the two craft were separated. *Eagle* then powered down to the Moon's surface.

Five minutes into *Eagle*'s descent the computer alarm went off. The team in Houston realised that this was not serious and instructed the astronauts to continue down to the Moon. The crew then realised that the computer was about to bring the *Eagle* to land in a large crater. Armstrong took matters into his own hands and steered the module away from disaster, using the last remaining fuel. After a tense few minutes he brought it down to land safely on the surface of the Moon, in an area called *Mare Tranquillitatis* (the Sea of Tranquility).

BUZZ ALDRIN ON THE MOON.

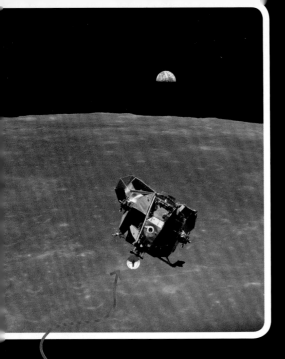

During his journey to the Moon, Armstrong took a moment to look back at the Earth. Afterwards he said: 'It suddenly struck me that the tiny pea, pretty and blue, was the Earth. I put up my thumb and shut one eye, and my thumb blotted out the planet Earth. I didn't feel like a giant. I felt very, very small.'

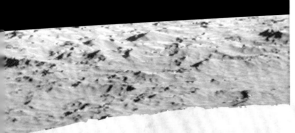

Have you ever been somewhere that makes you feel very small? Perhaps when you've looked out to sea or stood on top of a mountain, or maybe when you've looked out of the window of an aeroplane?

Six hours after landing, Armstrong finally set foot on the Moon's surface and said:

'That's one small step for man, one giant leap for mankind.'

BUZZ ALDRIN GAVE THIS DESCRIPTION OF THE MOON'S SURFACE A NUMBER OF YEARS LATER:
'The surface of the moon was like fine talcum powder ... When you put your foot down in the powder, the footprint preserved itself exquisitely... I'm trying the best I can to put it into words, but being on the moon is just different – different from anything you've ever seen. To use the word alien would mislead people. Surreal is probably as good a word as I have.'

Armstrong claims that he actually said 'a man' but the receivers in Houston didn't register this small word, so we all know his famous quote without the extra 'a'. It would actually be more surprising if all of the radio contact between the Moon and the Earth had been word perfect!

WHAT DID THEY EAT?

The astronauts ate 'space food' that had been dehydrated, which means the water had been taken out of it. They added hot water to the dried food before eating it with a spoon from a specially designed plastic container.

MOON FACTS

There is actually gravity on the Moon, it's just very low.
There is no rain or wind on the Moon, so a footprint left on its surface by those first astronauts is still there.
Only 12 people have ever walked on the Moon.

How did they survive in extreme conditions?

NASA describes its spacesuits as a 'one-person spacecraft'. This mission was the first in which the suits had to protect astronauts while walking on the moon, without being connected to a spacecraft. The boots had to be suitable for walking on a rocky surface and the suit had to contain a life-support system, which included its own supply of oxygen. Previous spacesuits had used a hose-like umbilical cord that connected the astronaut to the spacecraft's oxygen supply.

SCIENCE ON THE MOON

Like many explorers before them, Armstrong and Aldrin were not merely tourists. Their mission was to collect information and samples to help humankind learn about the Moon. For two-and-a-half hours they collected rock samples, set up experiments and tested out various ways of moving on the lunar surface in their cumbersome spacesuits. You can try out some moves yourself!

Kangaroo hop – jump forward on two legs.
Skipping – don't forget to hold your arms out for balance.
Galloping – apparently this was Buzz Aldrin's preferred method.

Aldrin preparing to remove the Early Apollo Scientific Experiments Package (EASEP) from its stowed position in the lunar module's scienfic bay.

Return to Earth

When their time on the Moon was up, Armstrong and Aldrin returned to *Eagle*, ascended back to orbit and docked with *Columbia* which was manned by Collins, the third crew member. It was in the small command module that the crew travelled back home. They re-entered Earth's atmosphere on 24 July 1969 and splash-landed in the Pacific Ocean. The astronauts then had to spend the next twenty-one days in quarantine just in case they had picked up any contagious diseases on the Moon.

THE INTERNATIONAL SPACE STATION.

So you want to be an explorer?

Have the stories of these explorers inspired you to get out there and see the world? Then it's time to plan your own adventure!

What kind of person makes a good explorer?

Anyone can be an explorer, but it certainly helps to have a thirst for adventure and the stamina to keep going when you come up against obstacles. Some explorers, like Ed Stafford, thrive on encountering danger because it breaks up the boredom of walking day after day after day on a long expedition.

ED STAFFORD

In 2008 Ed Stafford set out from the source of the Amazon River. His aim was to walk the entire length of the world's second longest river, which runs from high up in the Andes Mountains, through the vast and often impenetrable Amazon Rainforest to the Atlantic Ocean. The journey was to take him 860 days. In his expedition diary, after after lightning struck dangerously close to him and his companion, Cho, Stafford wrote:

'People often ask how we deal with the dangers: wading through waters inhabited by huge black caiman, stepping close to deadly pit vipers, or encountering fierce tribes. The honest answer is that these times are thrilling and exciting - time flies. They help distract us from the far more destructive phenomena - monotony and boredom.'

Why do you want to explore?

Darwin, Humbolt, Merian – what do those explorers have in common? They were all passionate about the natural world. This enthusiasm spurred them on to travel and discover as much as possible. Most modern-day explorers also have an interest in the world. They are keen to find out how it works, to learn about the plants and animals that inhabit our planet and to meet people from different cultures.

What are you passionate about?

Some modern-day explorers, such as Roz Savage, plan their adventures not only to challenge themselves mentally and physically but also to raise awareness about a cause close to their heart, such as the fragility of the planet we live on, or to raise money for their favourite charity.

GEORGE MCGAVIN

Explorer, entomologist and TV presenter George McGavin has taken part in numerous expeditions to places full of extraordinary animals. McGavin says that 'understanding the natural world is more important today than ever before – after all, we depend on all the other species on Earth for our own survival.'

He's spent five days in total darkness in a cave system in Venezuela, crawled into an 80ft-long hollow log at risk of being stung by scorpions and bitten by spiders, and he's had 80,000 bees swarming over him. McGavin has come out of these adventures unscathed but exhilarated after getting up close and personal with his beloved bugs. Along the way, the explorer has discovered a number of new species, including a spider in Borneo, a cockroach in Thailand and a cave cricket in Venezuela. McGavin has even had some species named after him. There are still about seven million species of insect in the world that have not yet been named and described – so why not get out there and start discovering!

ROZ SAVAGE

Roz Savage is the first woman to have rowed solo across three oceans – the Atlantic, Pacific and Indian. Her longest non-stop voyage was across the Indian Ocean from Australia to Mauritius, a journey of around 4,000 miles (6,400km). On her adventures, Savage has faced challenges such as mountainous seas (from which she had to be rescued by helicopter), being capsized constantly and nearly becoming separated from her boat after swimming to pick up something that dropped overboard. Savage is passionate about raising awareness of environmental issues and this mission has helped her through dark times. She says: 'When the going got tough, it really helped to have a huge reason WHY I was doing these ridiculously hard journeys.'

Illustration list